# Out and About

# Out and About

## Fifty Years *of* Wildlife Watching

Doug Gilroy

FIFTH HOUSE
PUBLISHERS

Front cover and interior photographs: Doug Gilroy
Front cover and interior illustrations: Jean Pilch, Calgary, Alberta
Cover and interior design: Brian Smith / Articulate Eye

The publisher gratefully acknowledges the support of the Department of Canadian Heritage and the Canada Council for the Arts for our publishing program.

The Canada Council for the Arts since 1957 | Le Conseil des Arts du Canada depuis 1957

We acknowledge the financial support of the Government of Canada through the Book Publishing Industry Development Program for our publishing activities.

Printed in Canada.

98 99 00 01 02 / 5 4 3 2 1

CANADIAN CATALOGUING IN PUBLICATION DATA

Gilroy, Doug, 1916–
Out and about

ISBN: 1-894004-07-8

1. Natural history Prairie Provinces. 2. Natural history Prairie Provinces Pictorial works. 3. Wildlife watching Prairie Provinces. 4. Gilroy, Doug, 1915 I. Title.

QH106.2.P6G538 1998 578'.09712 C98-910591-1

Fifth House Ltd.
#9 - 6125 11 St. SE
Calgary, AB, Canada
T2H 2L6

1-800-360-8826

# Contents

Welcome to the Wild . . . . . . . . . . 1
A Robin Builds Her Very First Nest . . . . . . . . . . 4
Hunters Love to Cook Up a Mallard . . . . . . . . . . 6
A Few Butterflies Came to Call . . . . . . . . . . 8
Slim Winter Pickings for Deer . . . . . . . . . . 11
Purple Cactus Blooms Look Like Jewels . . . . . . . . . . 14
A Baby Owl Becomes a Beloved Pet . . . . . . . . . . 17
Seeds Choose Different Modes of Transport . . . . . . . . . . 20
Shovelers Make a Long Migration . . . . . . . . . . 23
Waxwings Feast on Mountain Ash Berries . . . . . . . . . . 25
Owls Come in All Shapes and Sizes . . . . . . . . . . 28
Cats Like to Munch on Chipmunks . . . . . . . . . . 31
An Enchanting Winter Sky . . . . . . . . . . 34
Each Bird Species Builds a Distinctive Nest . . . . . . . . . . 36
Marshes Are Nature's Hideaway . . . . . . . . . . 39
Curious Weasels Make Great Mousers . . . . . . . . . . 42
Underwing Moths Blend In . . . . . . . . . . 45
How Do Gulls Find Food in the Snow? . . . . . . . . . . 47
Hawks and Kestrels Take to the Air . . . . . . . . . . 50
Autumn Leaves Drop and Winter Birds Return . . . . . . . . . . 53
Squirrels Scamper on the Highwire . . . . . . . . . . 56
Wild Geese Adore a Blueberry Patch . . . . . . . . . . 59
Nuthatches Can Be Comical Winter Guests . . . . . . . . . . 62
Skinning a Porcupine Is Hard Work . . . . . . . . . . 64
Colors Camouflage the Marbled Godwit . . . . . . . . . . 67
Insects Are Integral to Nature's Scheme . . . . . . . . . . 70
Masked Raccoons Rob at Night . . . . . . . . . . 72
BC Honors the Insatiable Jay . . . . . . . . . . 75

Mallard Drakes' Spring Plumage Is Majestic . . . . . . . . . . . . . . . . 78
Lady's Slippers Are Unique and Dainty . . . . . . . . . . . . . . . . . . . . 80
Thirsty Chipmunks Enjoy the Bird Bath . . . . . . . . . . . . . . . . . . . 82
Common Sora Rails Are Seldom Seen . . . . . . . . . . . . . . . . . . . . . 85
A Fly Can Be a Thing of Beauty . . . . . . . . . . . . . . . . . . . . . . . . 87
Striped Squirrels Disappear in Grass . . . . . . . . . . . . . . . . . . . . 90
Fireweed Flourishes Far and Wide . . . . . . . . . . . . . . . . . . . . . . 92
Grouse Scratch for Food in Tough Winters . . . . . . . . . . . . . . . . 95
Whistling Swans Pass through the Prairies . . . . . . . . . . . . . . . . 98
Pussywillows Herald Spring . . . . . . . . . . . . . . . . . . . . . . . . . . 100
The Northern Oriole's Origin . . . . . . . . . . . . . . . . . . . . . . . . . 102
Snowy Owls Winter in the South . . . . . . . . . . . . . . . . . . . . . . . 105
Magnificent Monarchs . . . . . . . . . . . . . . . . . . . . . . . . . . . . . . 111
The Bohemian Waxwing: Our Bird of Winter . . . . . . . . . . . . . . 114
Chicken and Duck Traits Mix in the Coot . . . . . . . . . . . . . . . . . 116
A Flicker Comes Close to Chilly Death . . . . . . . . . . . . . . . . . . . 119
Unhurried Hawks Fly South . . . . . . . . . . . . . . . . . . . . . . . . . . 122
Pintail Ducks Arrive Early . . . . . . . . . . . . . . . . . . . . . . . . . . . 125
Marsh Hawks Become Good Hunters . . . . . . . . . . . . . . . . . . . . 127
This Hare Wears Shoes and Changes Coats . . . . . . . . . . . . . . . 130
Wrens Stuff Twigs into Handy Spots . . . . . . . . . . . . . . . . . . . . 132
The Loon Sounds So Mournful and Wild . . . . . . . . . . . . . . . . . 134
Indian Paintbrush Bracts Provide Brilliant Color . . . . . . . . . . . 137
Butterflies Never Stay Still . . . . . . . . . . . . . . . . . . . . . . . . . . 140
Geese Spring to the Nest . . . . . . . . . . . . . . . . . . . . . . . . . . . 143
These Predators Enjoy Fresh Meat . . . . . . . . . . . . . . . . . . . . . 145
Pronghorns Were Once Near Extinction . . . . . . . . . . . . . . . . . . 148

# King of Columns

SHEILA ROBERTSON

Doug Gilroy likes to claim he was only 10 when he began writing his nature column for *The Western Producer* in 1954. He was, in fact, a young farmer, married with a small son. All these years later, garbed in jeans and sneakers, he is able, still, to scramble up snowbanks for a hike along the lakeside trail near his home at Regina Beach, Saskatchewan. He and Mary, his wife of 50 years, swim daily in Last Mountain Lake, spring through fall.

They have lived in the resort town since they retired from their farm in the nearby Lumsden area in 1973. "We always used to be the first to take a dip in the spring, and the last ones in the fall," he said. "We'd start the 24th of May, when there was still ice in the middle of the lake." He paused and grinned. "When you're young, you're nuts, you know."

Spry and wry, Gilroy belies his 82 years. Alert to the nuances of the seasons, and of plant, animal and insect life, Gilroy has been sharing his observations with readers through his regular column. It ran weekly for many years and now appears in *Western People* twice a month. With more than 1500 columns under his belt, Gilroy continues to write them longhand, and Mary types them.

His conversational columns have touched on topics ranging from purple finches and owls to tamarack trees and the nature of snow. One column starred a narcoleptic nuthatch that had inexplicably passed out under the Gilroys' suet feeder.

Gilroy is never at a loss for topics, even after all the columns he has written, but he stresses the importance of the interchange with his readers. Many comments are worked into columns, and he answers all the letters personally.

He enjoys reading the mail almost as much as taking his daily walks, during which he carries a camera and often adds to his collection of thousands of slides of the outdoors.

"There used to be a railroad right here," he explained, striding along the edge of the lake. "When they took up the track 10 years ago, they made it into a hiking trail. Part of it is paved, and in the summer I'm usually out here at 6 a.m. walking the dogs." Even when a colorful line of ice-fishing shacks strings across the lake's frozen expanse, there are creatures to watch for, he said.

With the exception of the barnyard chores, the rhythm of his days is not much different now from that of his boyhood on a dairy farm in the Boggy Creek Valley north of Regina. His interest in the natural world was supported by his parents, and he was always watching for birds and animals when heading out on horseback to get the cows.

"Dad loved nature, and he loved planting trees. Maybe I inherited that. He was also a good artist."

He joked about his failure to impart this fascination to his son, Greg. "When he was a little kid, he knew all the birds in the book, but now he calls me a crazy bird watcher. I tried to get him to come along on the Christmas bird count, but he said, 'No, I'm not going out there in the cold looking for a bunch of tweets.'" At this, both Gilroys chuckled.

He can pinpoint exactly when his long career began, at a slide presentation given by naturalist Dan McCowan in Regina in the late 1940s. "This fellow gave an illustrated lecture on Banff and the Rockies. It was the first time I'd ever seen color slides and they were so gorgeous, so beautiful!

"I made up my mind right then that I wanted to do the same thing. I bought a camera, and started building up a collection. Pretty soon, I was being invited to give slide shows."

He learned photography and writing by trial and error, he said. He paid $5 for his first color-capable camera, a Kodak Bantam F-8, which used 12-shot rolls of 10 ASA film. Now he has two Pentax cameras and a range of lenses. A favorite for close-ups is a 100-mm short-barreled telephoto incorporating a bellows extension device.

As a result of his presentations and his articles for *Blue Jay*, the magazine of the Saskatchewan Natural History Society, the Regina Board of Education asked Gilroy to present biannual slide lectures on the outdoors. "I'd give the classes a bit of a nature tour, talking about the crocuses, the birds coming back, the frogs." He continued to do this for 17 years.

Other media sought out his expertise. "I remember the first time I was on CBC Radio," he said. "I was scared half to death." To make matters worse, the show's host was less than encouraging.

"When we finished, he said, 'That was terrible; you slurred some words, you mispronounced some others.' Yet they used it; my sister heard the interview in Vancouver." He realized, though, that his future probably wasn't in broadcasting.

Meanwhile, a contact with the Natural History Society had given his name to *The Western Producer*, which was looking for someone to write a weekly nature column. "This was what I'd always wanted to do, so I thought I'd give it a try."

Rusty McDonald, then executive editor, gave Gilroy some initial advice that served him well. "He said, 'Don't try to be fancy; just be natural.'"

McDonald also advised him to take advantage of reader input. "He told me to be sure to use their names. Readers like to see their names in print."

He remembers the first letter he received, from an Elfros, Saskatchewan, reader named Jessie Cameron. Over 43 years, there have been too many respondents to know them all by name, but he certainly recalls the situations some of them related.

"A reader in Prince Albert, Saskatchewan, wrote about bluebirds building a nest of nails. And then there was a lady from Pincher Creek, Alberta, who would put food out for this family of skunks that came to her house. She fed them out of the dog's dish. It backfired, though, when her grandson was home alone and left a door open. He heard a rustling in the kitchen and discovered a houseful of skunks."

If asked questions he can't answer, Gilroy turns to his wide circle of contacts. Recently, he had to research the origins of the caragana for a curious reader.

Gilroy's house is full of enlargements of his wildlife photos. They include a picture of a raccoon that had been raiding the bird feeder in the middle of the night; a chipmunk; pincherries; a pelican; and a spectacular sundog glistening in the winter sky.

Gilroy has had four books published by Western Producer Prairie Books. The first, *An Album of Prairie Birds*, appeared in 1967.

Having closely surveyed wildlife since his youth, Gilroy is passionate about the need to conserve places for wild creatures. "I'm concerned about the destruction of the natural habitats, especially the clearcutting of trees and draining of the wetlands," he said. "I hate to see all the native prairie being plowed up, and farmers planting right up to the ditches."

This is a rare outburst. Gilroy prefers to let his pictures speak for him.

Reprinted courtesy *The Western Producer*

# Welcome to the Wild

The Western chipmunk has a nervous manner.

A few miles north of Regina a small creek winds its way in a southwesterly direction across the broad, flat wheatlands. Until it reaches Condie dam it is not much of a creek at all. Some places it is merely a trickle, and at other places dries up completely.

After leaving Condie dam it continues on its way, a little more vigorous perhaps, but still not making much of an attempt to become a river. Gradually trees begin to appear along its banks; at first, only a few scrubby willows, then chokecherries and saskatoons. The willows become thicker, and larger trees such as Manitoba maple, ash, elm and poplar come into view. With the appearance of the larger trees, the little ravine the creek followed has suddenly become much wider and deeper. It has rapidly become a surprisingly beautiful valley, with broad, flat meadowlands and heavily treed, steep side-hills and coulees.

The little creek and valley continue in a twisty sort of way for eight miles. Here it joins the great Qu'Appelle Valley, and the creek's waters flow into the Qu'Appelle River. The name of this creek is Boggy Creek, and the valley is called Boggy Creek Valley.

Many people will ask why it is called "Boggy" Creek. For one thing, it has little or no gravel on the bottom, and if one were to walk into it he would more than likely sink up to his knees in mud. For another reason, it is spring fed, and wherever there are springs there is usually quite a lot of bog and muskeg. There are several places along the banks where there are regular little swamps, and if you jump, the ground will bob up and down for several feet all around you. So Boggy Creek is very well named.

My farm home is located along the creek at the beginning of Boggy Creek Valley. It is from this point that I take hikes and make a great many of my nature observations and indulge in my favorite hobby—nature photography. This region and the surrounding country is second to none for those wishing to study the native wildlife and botany.

Take the dryland animals, for instance. If one were to walk back into the wooded ravines on a quiet winter day, he would suddenly be startled by the cracking of dead sticks and looking up see a fine buck go bounding over the ridge.

We have two species of deer here in Boggy Creek Valley—the "mule deer" and "white tail." A few years ago I have on many occasions seen as many as 30 in one herd. That was when there was a closed season on deer. Now that we've had a few years of open season they have been depleted considerably but are still quite common.

Dropping from the largest mammal to the smallest, the common shrew—in fact it is the smallest mammal in North America—the tracks of this busy little fellow can be seen where he has run lightly over the snow and suddenly disappeared down an ever-so-small hole that he himself made when he decided to travel under instead of over in his everlasting search for food. He has no time to sleep all winter as many other small animals do, for Mother Nature has made him so he must eat almost continually. In fact, if he has to go without food for only a few hours, he will die of starvation.

This little mite, however, is by no means a rarity. Hundreds of people all over Canada have shrews in their own back yard and do not even know it.

Among the small animal folk of Boggy Creek my favorite is the Western chipmunk. This spry little fellow can often be seen regarding you from his perch on a tall branch and nervously jerking his tail to and fro as he decides to scamper off to a safer distance.

Red squirrels can be seen on occasion as well as the Franklin's ground squirrel or bush gopher, which is very common. His first cousin, the thirteen-lined ground squirrel, inhabits the prairie land in fair number. Being shy, he is not seen as often as his bolder relatives.

Many narrow parts of the creek have now become very broad because beavers have moved in and built dams, raising the water considerably. This higher water naturally attracts waterfowl and muskrats.

Four members of the weasel family are found in this territory—badger, skunk, mink and weasel. In the summer a stranger rarely sees weasel and mink, especially the latter, but as soon as the first snow appears one has no trouble at all finding their tracks. So they are here in greater numbers than one might think.

Porcupine is common in the valley. I won't go into detail about the bird life of Boggy Creek, as it would take up too great a space, but I will deal with them in future columns. I would like to mention, though, that 70 species have been counted nesting here, ranging from sora rails and ducks to woodpeckers and great blue herons.

**Doug Gilroy wrote this column, his first, for the 7 January 1954 issue of *The Western Producer***

# A Robin Builds Her Very First Nest

Mother robin lay on her side to pack the nest with her feet.

The sky seems much bluer now and the clouds are starting to get big and fluffy—like chunks of whipped cream or cotton batting. To me a plain blue cloudless sky looks so empty; it takes clouds to make it interesting. So many western storytellers write of the great dome of the western sky, and of course the blazing sunsets.

But once again we need a certain amount of clouds above the horizon to reflect the red and orange rays of the setting sun to make it really beautiful.

Our lake is free of ice again, and how good it is to see that stretch of open blue water. Flocks of gulls are flying over its surface, often following the shore line to land on the rocks where they talk and argue among themselves.

Back in late March, the first robins began to appear and by April they were singing their early morning song to welcome a brand new day.

By now, many have mated and nest building has begun. My picture shows a robin snuggled down in her newly built nest in a spruce tree. She and her mate worked hard to build that nest, gathering vegetable matter and mud to make a solid, firm cup inside.

To shape it she would lie on her side and kick and pack it with her feet to get the exact shape. Then more grass and plant fibre were used to upholster it to make it soft for the blue eggs that would soon follow.

She was hatched last year and this was the first nest she had ever built, yet she knew exactly how to make it. I guess we humans would call it instinct. Sadly, the nest was destroyed by crows a few days after the picture was taken.

It's always a thrill to see the first crow in spring, but when they come into the yard to destroy the nests of smaller birds, the use of a shotgun comes to mind. But it's against the law to fire a gun in this resort town.

Robins and bluebirds are quite closely related; both belonging to the thrush family.

**These greenhead mallards can stay all winter on Regina's Wascana Lake.**

# *Hunters Love to Cook Up a Mallard*

My picture today features a flock of ducks, mostly greenhead mallards. This picture was taken in winter in Regina. Warm water from the old power station on Wascana Lake would keep an area of the lake open and ducks and geese would spend the winter there rather than fly south.

Of all the ducks species, the mallard is a favorite for hunters. It's a large duck and makes an excellent table bird. Unfortunately, biologists say its population is declining at an alarming rate. According to an article in the Regina *Leader-Post*, there were 11 million mallard ducks nesting in Saskatchewan in 1976. At the spring count a few years ago, they were down to about four million. Other species such as pintails were also down.

Drought, dried-up wetlands and loss of habitat have all contributed to the situation.

It is believed that ducks won't breed when forced out of their habitual nesting area, even if water and habitat are restored in other areas. They have to start over again the following year.

When farmers clear the upland areas, they are further exposing ducks and other species of birds to predators. Nests are destroyed and breeding interrupted.

With the great decline in ducks, it seems reasonable to cut down on hunting limits or even eliminate one duck hunting season for one or two years in Canada and the United States.

Give the ducks a chance.

We are now one week into February, the month when the great-horned owls start to nest. Their mating hoots and shrieks do much to liven up a cold moonlit night. Romantic? It sure is, if you are an owl.

# A Few Butterflies Came to Call

The thistle butterfly love marigolds, as well as thistles.

We have had a fairly good selection of butterflies visiting our yard this year. It seems to me that there were not as many as in other years. I suppose they come and go in cycles.

It started off with one or two of the tiny little blue species. Along with the blues there were two or three tiny brown butterflies belonging to a species called coppers. A mourning cloak (a weird name for a butterfly) also appeared quite early. This butterfly is a hibernator, one of the few that sleeps over winter as an adult. It is reputed to have one of the longest lifespans for a butterfly in North America; it lives up to eight months. It is black or dark brown with a border of whitish fawn around the edge of its wings.

We also had several red admirals as well as one white admiral. The main identification mark of the red admiral is the orange-red band that passes through the upper third of its dark wings. This is another hibernator that winters over. I remember lifting up a log out of the snow one winter and to my surprise two red admirals were attached to the underside.

Several fritillaries fluttered around the yard in June. There was also a tiger swallowtail, easily recognized by its large size and the prominent tails on the hind wing, which resemble the forked tail of barn swallows. In Ontario there is a black swallowtail. (I would love to see one of these.)

A yellow sulphur butterfly paid us a call, as well as a common white cabbage butterfly. We haven't any cabbages, but nevertheless it called in to see if we had.

In late June one satyr angel wing lit on the tip of a spruce branch, but it is the only one that has called in so far.

My photo today features a very lovely specimen known as the painted lady or thistle butterfly. It may like thistle blossoms, but around my place it really loves marigolds, where I photographed it using closeup equipment. The smell of marigolds isn't too appealing to humans, but apparently it is to certain butterflies.

It is said that the painted lady butterfly is the most widespread butterfly in the world. It is a migrator, and in the spring it travels as far as 3100 miles.

Lorraine Johnson of Lucky Lake, Saskatchewan, sent me a lovely picture of an oriole sipping nectar from a hummingbird feeder. It used to be, as far as I know, an uncommon occurrence. But in the last number of years it has become quite common. The orioles weren't slow in catching on to a good thing, and even the chickadees take a few sips of nectar.

In the spring lots of people will hang out strips of yarn for the orioles to collect for nesting material. Bernice Sprague of Wolseley, Saskatchewan, wrote that her young beagle is tied by a 15-foot rope to the corner of their house, where it had a fun time wrestling a scrap of carpet to tatters. Some of the crinkly fibers became entangled in the rope.

"Early one morning when my husband was at work in our upholstery shop in our back yard, he noticed an industrious little female goldfinch trying to retrieve these fibres. To save her from what was an impossible task he plucked a wad of cotton padding from the bale we keep on hand for use in the shop and snagged it to the rope. She wasn't long discovering it and made many return trips to the tuft of cotton, the carpet threads forgotten."

Speaking of goldfinches, these bright yellow birds with black wings seem to be in great abundance this year, and robins too. There have been more robins around than we have had for quite some time.

A. L. Clark of Moosomin, Saskatchewan, writes: "Yesterday and today I was seeding and saw twelve or fourteen birds in two flocks that would merge and separate. The birds were the size of and had similar habits to mourning doves. They had black heads with large white patches on each side, the breasts were dark grey or black and the wings were grey. The six or seven bird flocks would fly in unison and search for bugs on the worked land."

I would say that these were black-bellied plovers. I used to see them out in the fields in the spring just as you did. They were on their way to their nesting ground up in the Arctic. They nest on the tundra.

# Slim Winter Pickings for Deer

With the snow and freezing rain this winter, the deer are having a rough time. In the valleys and coulees the snow is so deep that in some places it is almost impossible for them to browse. Many take to the stubble fields, but even there the snow is deep and crusted, making it difficult for them to paw down to find any edible grain.

Officials claim many deer will become so weakened they will die before spring. Under such conditions, hungry deer invade haystacks and do damage. However, some kind-hearted farmers feel sorry for the deer and each day put out a little grain. The deer feeding in the photograph are white-tails.

Speaking of winter, 19th-century writer Christina Georgina Rossetti writes that in winter the earth appears lifeless and without hope. It seems nothing can withstand the harshness of the season.

"Yet, in the midst of winter we see standing the evergreen making its declaration for life ongoing and forward looking. Like a messenger of hope, struggling through a storm, the evergreen, crusted with frost and snow, stretches out its limbs. It offers shelter and food to the birds of the air and those animals who can huddle under its branches. The evergreen is truly a sign of hope for today."

In an earlier column, I wrote about the tamarack tree. Inspired by this, Carl J. Osterberg of Shaunavon, Saskatchewan, sent in the following report.

"My wife and I lived for 20 years in the United States. Eight of those years we lived in the beautiful Flathead Valley, Kalispell area of Montana. We are familiar with the tamarack tree.

"When we first arrived in late November and saw the forest with all those yellowish, dead-looking trees, our thoughts were—what destruction by insects. We learned, however, that they were very much alive and sprouted in the spring into a beautiful lush green, soft to the touch. The tamarack is endemic to that area.

"My experience with the tamarack is not with the live tree but with the dead one. It is prime firewood, burns very hot and is much sought after. We lived in the wilderness and our source of heat was the wood stove.

"For our own use we cut five cords of wood for winter. However, the last five years, to supplement our income, I cut down a tree, split the wood and loaded one cord of wood on the truck, then sold it in Kalispell. It was really hard work without the heavy equipment some woodcutters had to make the job faster and easier.

"Every year after that I sold 25 cords in town and could never supply enough for my customers. In the forest hundreds of dead tamaracks would stand like silent cathedrals. Most of them were very wide at the bottom and demanded a lot of respect when contemplating cutting them down. The vibration of the chain saw would make the top portion of the tree come down like an arrow. I once got two cords out of one tree and still had 25 feet left over."

Freda Markland of Melfort, Saskatchewan, wrote to tell of some of her summer memories, including a cruise on the Saskatchewan River. Under the Gronlid bridge, she saw many bottle-like nests of cliff swallows. In the immediate area were several plastic owls. She wonders why they were put there and why anyone would want to interfere with the swallows. On the cruise she also saw many pelicans, terns and cormorants.

At a neighbor's auction sale, she found a nest of wrens in a grain auger. The new owner had a kind heart and left the auger until the young wrens left the nest.

Purple finches invaded Markland's yard and enjoyed a diet of canola, flax and broken sunflower seeds. In November, Bohemian waxwings visited her mountain ash tree and cleaned up on the berries. Often a diet of frozen mountain ash berries makes waxwings appear intoxicated. It must affect their nervous systems.

About 200 evening grosbeaks arrived November 23 to visit her feeders and to clean up the sunflower seeds. About the same time, a small flock of redpolls showed up, as well as two pine grosbeaks.

Pine grosbeaks don't seem to go after sunflower seeds in the same manner as evening grosbeaks. They are more fruit and berry eaters, but do enjoy the seeds they extract from pine and spruce cones. They have also been seen feeding on the seed heads of flax that protrude above the snow.

White-tail deer must look hard for food when the snow is deep.

# Purple Cactus Blooms Look Like Jewels

May 24 has come and gone. When I was a kid, it was a big day: a sports day, the first swim of the year day and planting the potatoes day. We at school would sing, "The 24th of May is the Queen's birthday. If you don't give us a holiday, we will all run away."

By then, most of the trees were out in full leaf, birds were nesting and young squirrels were out exploring the tree world for the first time. Now, the blooming of the early spring flowers such as the prairie crocus, golden peas and moss phlox have come and gone and are now in the seed stage.

But many more are yet to come. My picture today shows the flower buds of the purple or ball cactus. Watch for it in late June on dry sunny hillsides. When in full bloom, its beauty is pretty hard to beat. The rich purplish red flowers, which so often come in a clump, resemble jewels in the grass.

Sometimes the flowers vary in color; some may be pinkish. Once I found a clump where the flowers were distinctly silver in color but I've never seen it since.

After the blooms have faded, a plump gooseberry-like fruit develops that is real tasty to eat. Although I have never tried it, I am told it makes excellent jam. The berries are easy to pick, you just simply lift them out. No need to get your fingers prickled.

Some interesting letters have arrived lately. Readers ask questions that I can't always answer so I have to do research and learn as we go along. We live in a wonderful world of nature and it is so good to share its delights with one another.

A good example is a letter about snakes and wasps from L. Snyder of Victoria, British Columbia. He writes: "Many years ago we lived on the edge of a small stream that ran through a bit of property on which we had a few sheep. Since the banks of the stream were a prime breeding ground for the common garter snake, there were literally thousands of the crawly creatures over the pasture where the sheep grazed.

"One day I noticed one of these small snakes all curled up and then it would strike the sheep on its nose. These are non-poisonous, harmless snakes, but they do know how to wind and strike just as a rattler does. The snakes were so numerous one could not walk without stepping on them. One day I had killed about 20 of them, throwing them into a post hole. But after I hit one that did not wiggle away, it looked at me with such sad eyes I couldn't destroy any more, even though the ground was alive with them. So like all animals, some are good and some are mean, but I would never have believed garter snakes had traits like the rattler if I had not witnessed it.

"Another bit of nature drama I witnessed one year with wasps. After I had swatted one on the window sill another one zeroed in on it and proceeded to cut off the wings and legs, then flew off with the body. Real cannibals."

Here is another letter from Irma Noden of New Norway, Alberta.

"One winter, Doug, my husband, had put some sunflower seeds in an old wooden box in a maple tree. The squirrel had a winter supply of spruce cones stored in the box. Blue Jay came along and tossed out the cones and fed on the sunflower seeds. When the jay had his fill and left, the squirrel would run all the cones up the tree and back into the box. This went on every morning of the winter. They never seemed to get tired of the game." Irma concludes this was great entertainment and well worth the price of the bird seed.

She says ruby-throated hummingbirds are a real delight and recalls moving the feeder one year to a new place. But when the hummingbirds came back the next spring, they went to the exact spot where the feeder had been previously. They flew around that area looking for it and seemed confused that it wasn't there.

I have had the very same experience myself. My hummer did exactly the same things as Irma's did when I moved my feeder from the crabapple tree to another location. This proves that birds are anything but dumb and have good memories.

This purple cactus, sporting gorgeous June blooms, will soon develop gooseberry-like fruit.

Two grosbeaks meet for a Yuletide smooch.

# A Baby Owl Becomes a Beloved Pet

Christmas is only a week away. Santa will be packing his bag and his deer will be having their hooves trimmed. Rudolf will be getting a new bulb and batteries installed in his nose so it will light up nice and red.

When I was a boy Santa never had a deer by the name of Rudolf. He came later. I suppose the red nose helps as a beacon so that other flying objects such as airplanes and geese won't fly into the sleigh.

This is my opportunity to wish my readers a very Merry Christmas. The picture I chose especially for this season shows two evening grosbeaks touching the ends of their bills together. They are either kissing or fighting. Surely they wouldn't quarrel during the Yuletide season, so let's assume they are kissing. I took the picture from a blind on a December day using a 250 mm lens.

Great horned owls will be active Christmas Eve but will roost quietly on the sheltered branch of a tree Christmas Day. At dusk they will once again hunt the snowy landscape for a Christmas supper.

Alfred Stanley of Clandonald, Alberta, sent in this owl story:

"When I was a lad in the spring of about 1942, my cousin and I played hooky from school and on our saddle horses rode to an unfenced quarter-section of poplar bush land. There, in a tall poplar tree, we discovered an owls' nest complete with Mom and Dad owls and babies. With much moral support from me, my cousin climbed the tree with the owls diving and narrowly missing him.

"He arrived safely back on the ground with two tiny white balls of fluff tucked under his cap on top of his head. He left two in the nest. George's owl lived only a week or two. My owl, Ollie, survived and thrived. I kept him, or it, in an old unused smoke house near our house.

"He grew to be a great pet for me, my sisters and mother. He always feared and disliked my father. The feeling was rather mutual. He would spread his wings, bob his head and make popping and hissing noises with his beak when Dad came near. My mother and I fed him small scraps of raw meat. As fall came I would go to the field where the men were loading grain stocks, and with the help of my dear dog, Mickey, we would catch large quantities of field mice, which I would store. Ollie would swallow them whole, head first, until the tail finally disappeared. I should state that early in the summer we would leave the door of his house open during the day and he went where he so desired. Amazingly Ollie never bothered our chickens.

"Late that fall, Mother, my three older sisters and I moved to Clandonald, 14 miles away, so my sisters could attend high school. This made Ollie unhappy, as he still would never allow Dad to feed him or go near. By now he had complete freedom to come and go where and when he wished. When we could make it to the farm Mother or I would call and he would answer sometimes 500 yards away. He would come immediately and show his affection by gently nibbling our fingers. If he were frightened or angry he would make the bill popping noise much louder. He had the most adorable huge yellow eyes and could swivel his head it seemed like 360 degrees.

"As spring drew near he would answer from farther away and sometimes not at all. Eventually he did not return. Thirty years passed. We still live on and farm the same land. When one of my daughters was about 15 years old she caught a baby horned owl, feathered but too young to fly. Ruby enjoyed him, or her, as a pet until she returned him to his natural habitat in a coulee on the farm.

"Over the years I have seen a great horned owl on many different occasions on our farm. Many times he would land on a tree near me.

"One evening last winter just after dark we were disturbed by the barking of our dog. Stepping outside there was no mistaking the frantic squawks coming from our chicken house. When my son and I went to investigate we discovered that one pane of glass had been pushed in. I had bales stacked outside almost to the bottom of the window. Mr. Great Horned Owl had removed the head from one hen, and was peacefully enjoying his supper in the far corner.

"We plugged the window and gently opened the door. 'Owl' hopped up on a roost. He carefully looked at the plugged window with his beautiful huge yellow eyes. He then looked us over with no visible sign of fear or excitement. I am sorry to say I was too stupid or dumb-founded to try calling Ollie, or even just talk to him.

"After taking pictures we opened the wide door. Mr. Owl's roost was about two feet off the floor. After studying the open door and the black dark outside for a couple of seconds 'Owl' gently swooped down, partially closing his wing span, and tipping sideways he flew out the door. He flew to and perched on the shop roof about 100 yards away, where we watched him by flashlight for a few minutes. Then he flew off into the night.

"The next morning he came and sat on our house roof for about 10 minutes. I have many times regretted not banding Ollie those many years ago. Since, it has been documented that great horned owls live for at least 40 years. I will always wonder if last winter's not unwelcome visitor was truly my Ollie."

It could be the same owl.

# Seeds Choose Different Modes of Transport

The sow thistle, displaying both flower and seed, is notorious.

The last two times I sat down to write a column it was raining chipmunks and hammer handles. Today, for a change, it is bright and sunny. What a relief to see blue sky.

The trees are more denuded of their leaves, but when I look around I'm surprised to see how many are left on certain species. The aspen poplars still have their leaves; most are yellow, but some still have a greenish tinge. This is also true of my Siberian elms and the willows down by the lake. A few lovely red leaves remain on the chokecherries, and the rose bushes are bright red. The lilac bushes are still fairly green;

they are among the last to go, whereas ash and Manitoba maple are about the first around these parts.

My photograph today is an excellent example of a plant in flower and in seed. This particular plant isn't popular with farmers, or anyone else for that matter, for it is the notorious sow thistle. There are three species of sow thistle, and the species pictured is the common perennial sow thistle, found most often in wet areas.

The seed heads look similar to those of the common dandelion. Each little seed is equipped with a light, fuzzy parachute, which at a certain ripe stage is caught by a breeze or strong wind. Away they go to land some distance away from the mother plant and grow again.

It is surprising the number of plant species that distribute their seeds in this way. Others have different methods. Some, for example, have burrs that stick to the fur of animals and even on the clothes of people; the blue burr is one of these plants.

The seeds of some trees, including poplars and willows, are equipped with little parachutes. Other tree seeds, such as ash and maple, are equipped with a wing. When they are blown off they go whirling away to drop some distance to the ground. The seeds of spruce and pine also have a tiny wing and travel in the same manner.

It is surprising the number of us who have never seen an evergreen seed. They are located under the scales of the cone and we never see them unless we get a cone at a certain stage. Then they can be shaken out in your hand or on a piece of paper.

Shirley D. Hoffman of Spalding, Saskatchewan, wrote to tell us of a strange happening.

"It had been a very hot day in July; however, the evening had become pleasantly cool and very still. My husband, Leo, was working outside by the garage when he stopped to listen to a strange snapping sound that seemed far away, yet close by. Walking towards the noise brought him to the grain dryer. The sound was coming from the right-hand corner down inside the dryer. After listening to the distinctive sound, Leo said, 'It sounds like an owl.'

"Climbing to the top of the dryer he looked in. Sure enough an owl was trapped in a compartment about 16 feet down that had no access to it.

"Concerned about getting the frightened bird out alive and unharmed, Leo said, 'Don't tell me I have to cut a hole in the dryer.' After thinking the situation over, and a couple of unsuccessful attempts to free the owl, he came up with the idea of lowering down an old freezer basket; however, it was too large. But as luck would have it by turning the basket on its side it would fit.

"Attaching a long rope to the basket he lowered it ever so very slowly until it reached the owl. Surprisingly the bird was not so frightened by this time, and for some strange reason it jumped into the basket, clenching itself tightly to the wires. Quickly, Leo pulled the basket as close as possible to the inside of the dryer to prevent the owl from falling out.

"Slowly and gently he pulled the poor trapped bird to the top. When the basket reached the top it came level with a flat platform. The owl jumped onto this platform and sat as if it were dazed by the bright light. After a few moments it flew away to the freedom of the sky. Yes, indeed, the bird was a large adult horned owl.

"It has been puzzling to us how this would have happened to an owl that is known for its great precision in hunting. The owl has seemed to say, 'Thank you for your kindness,' for we see our new friend most evenings perched in the grove of trees just a short way from the grain dryer. We are very pleased to know the owl feels safe enough to call our farm home."

How the bird got in there is indeed a question. Somehow the owl must have lost its grip when landing there and slid all the way down.

Your husband deserves a medal for his kindness and thoughtfulness in rescuing that owl. It also seems the owl knew efforts were being made for its rescue, and knew enough to jump in that basket to be lifted out. Who said birds are dumb?

# Shovelers Make a Long Migration

A northern shoveler drake is featured on the page this week. Both female and male shovelers can be easily recognized by their large, spoon-shaped bill. In fact, around duck hunting groups at this time of year, this species of duck is often called the spoonbill.

The dress of male shovelers in late autumn and spring resembles that of drake mallards except for the head, which is more greenish black. Both male and female shovelers have blue wing patches that resemble those of the blue-winged teal.

When little shoveler ducklings are first hatched, their beaks are the same as other little ducks, but this changes quickly and they become spoon-shaped in a matter of two or three weeks.

Shovelers are warm weather ducks; they don't hang around till late fall as the mallards and some others do before heading south. They winter as far south as Central America and the West Indies. It is claimed that some of the hardy ones cross the 2000 miles of ocean to Hawaii.

Mrs. E. Mackie of Margo, Saskatchewan, sent in a couple of drawings of a bird that would come to an almost dry slough near her home for a week back in mid-June. She said it would arrive every morning around 8:30 and feed on frogs until five or six p.m. Then it would fly away for the night.

She said it was about the size of a mallard duck, light grey with blue-black on back and head. It had bright red eyes and orange colored legs. She said it did not swim, but when alarmed it flew and perched in a tree.

From her descriptions plus the drawings she sent, which are very good, it can't be anything else but a black-crowned night heron. This species will nest in colonies, usually in trees, but sometimes on the ground in marshy areas. It's a cousin to the great blue heron, which also nests in colonies in trees.

Here is a letter from Mrs. Katie Thompson of Bangor, Saskatchewan. She writes: "I have read all your columns and get a great deal of pleasure from bird watching. I usually have many visitors at my bird bath all summer especially goldfinches, robins, catbirds, wrens and always hummingbirds among the petunias.

"One morning I had the sprinkler on and 14 bluebirds flew back and forth in the spray. One pair nested on a ledge under the eaves.

"That was last year. I had none this summer.

"Early this spring a pair of birds, strangers to me, nested in my spruce windbreak. Later one Sunday a man called in; he was Adam Smith of Melville, Saskatchewan. He played a recording of a bird's voice and asked if I recognized it. I did and it was the voice of my new birds. It went "Ki, Ki, Ki, Ki, Ki, Ki." He said that they were merlin hawks, also known as pigeon hawks. I told him they were nesting in my yard and he asked permission to band them. I said, 'OK, but don't hurt them.' Now that I know their bad habits I wish I had paid him to wring their little necks. They are death on songbirds, and no wonder I did not have bluebirds this summer—my yard was only occupied by barn swallows and grasshoppers."

The merlin is a small falcon slightly bigger than the sparrow hawk or kestrel. It nests in trees or bushes in old nests of other large birds. I found one once in an old magpie nest. It breeds in Alaska and across Canada to the northern United States.

Like all falcons the merlin requires fresh food, which it captures on the fly, such as small birds, dragonflies and grasshoppers. If they are not disturbed they are quite quiet, but protest loudly when their territory is intruded upon. It is said that in the fall, migrating sandpipers around sloughs are a common prey.

Shovelers winter as far south as Central America and the West Indies.

# Waxwings Feast on Mountain Ash Berries

Mountain ash berries, wrongly rumored to be poisonous, actually make tasty jelly.

Mountain ash berries are favored by wild birds during the winter, especially by the waxwings, both the Bohemian and cedar varieties. But as the Bohemian is the waxwing commonly seen during the cold season, it will benefit from the berries most. However, repeated thawing and freezing of the berry creates a substance that has a strange effect on the birds if they partake of too many berries. They act drugged. Some say drunk, although I rather doubt the berries possess any alcohol content. But it does seem to affect the nervous system.

The mountain ash is also known as the Rowan tree. There are several species in North America. One or two are native, and the others are imports from Europe, North Africa, Japan and Scandinavia. Many of us have the idea that the berries of mountain ash are poisonous, but such is not the case. The fruit, particularly of the American mountain ash, is tart, rich in vitamins and makes excellent jelly. The berries are also used in herbal remedies.

One species that is termed exotic is the European mountain ash. It is widely planted as an ornamental in this country and with the help of birds has escaped into the wild, giving the impression that it is a native tree. As far as I am concerned the species are hard to identify or separate. However, if one attempts to try to identify the kind in their yard this hint might help.

The European mountain ash (or Rowan tree) can possibly be recognized by its winter buds, which are not gummy but densely covered with white, woolly hairs. The fruit is larger than with native species and looks quite pulpy. More than likely the one in my picture, which I photographed in my own yard, is of this species. The wood of the mountain ashes has no commercial value; they are not true ashes. They often grow with two or more trunks. A healthy, well-formed tree, loaded with scarlet berries, is indeed a beautiful sight in the fall.

The days are a little longer now. The movement of wild birds, and even mammals to a certain extent, are said to be affected by the changing hours of daylight. We have lots of chickadees, hairy and downy woodpeckers, and one or two magpies, and a white-breasted nuthatch has been calling in on the odd day. But so far we have had no blue jays, evening grosbeaks, waxwings or snowy owls. A single redpoll called in one day but then disappeared.

Every winter I get a report of a certain summer species dropping in at somebody's feeding station, and this winter is no exception. Irene Vivian of White Fox, Saskatchewan, writes: "I enjoy your column very much. In late November we had an oriole eating at the feeder with the evening grosbeaks. The chickadees and grosbeaks would chase it away, but it would soon return. It seemed to like scratching on the ground. It was quite cold at that time, dropping down to -20°F, and the oriole would fluff up its feathers to keep warm. We have blue jays that visit our feeder daily, and also a pileated woodpecker has been seen several times."

Mrs. Vivian lives on a farm, and she remarked that several of her neighbors have feeding stations as well, and that is good. It not only helps the birds of the district, but also provides a lot of entertainment for the provider. These wild creatures are great company. If one has them coming, and then suddenly they don't come anymore, it is lonely without them.

Mrs. Vivian wrote of a mirage and a sun dog display that she saw last winter. She said in the mirage the whole field across to White Fox was lifted up high.

There are some most interesting sights to be seen in winter. As she remarked, sundogs gleaming like objects of brass are out of this world if one stops to look at them. To photograph them one needs a 28 mm wide-angle lens.

Hello to Joan Wootton at Bo-Peep's Place at Langley, British Columbia. A friend of hers, Glenn Ryder, a prominent naturalist writer in British Columbia, found two nests of the Rufous hummingbird in Campbell Creek Valley Park. He collected them after the young had left the nest, of course. Joan Wootton sent them on to me, along with a little anecdote.

She said that many years ago she took a little hummingbird's nest next door to the neighbor's visiting grandchildren. To make it look more realistic she put two white navy beans in the nest. The five-year-old said, "Granny, I know those are real eggs because one has a crack in it."

Hello to Mrs. W. G. Smith of Bulyea, Saskatchewan. She says that back in the good old summertime a little wild canary was injured by a young lad with an air gun. One of its wing tips was damaged, and she felt the tip was gone. However, she carefully nursed it and fed it all the wild seeds and a few tame varieties such as canary seeds. It is now a household pet. At last report it was doing well except that one day it struggled in a hurry to get out of her husband's hand when her husband was holding its tail a little harder than he realized. It is now tail-less. Mrs. Smith wonders if the tail will grow back in by spring.

I am quite sure that it will. Mother Nature is usually pretty good at replacing missing tail feathers.

Mrs. Smith says the little canary is very knowledgeable but is still as wild as when she got him. It's interesting to watch him bathing in the fruit dish. She says the water must be sparkling clean. Fussy little thing, isn't he!

# Owls Come in All Shapes and Sizes

Great horned owls—this is a young one—can kill a full-grown turkey.

The smallest owl on the prairies is the saw-whet owl, about the size of a man's clenched fist. It is followed closely by the boreal owl, which likes to nest in hollow trees like the saw-whet.

Then comes the burrowing owl, which nests in holes in the ground. The screech owl is probably next in size, nesting in tree cavities.

Next is the hawk owl found in big timber country. With its longer tail, it looks like a cross between a hawk and an owl. It uses a discarded nest of a raven or hawk.

The long-eared owl is about the size of a crow. Its plumage is of soft wood-brown colors and is named for the two feather tufts that protrude from the head resembling long ears. Happy to use last year's crow's nest to lay its five to seven pure white eggs, it is found in wooded valleys and coulees.

About the same size as the long-eared owl is the short-eared owl. It likes the grassy prairie, where it lays its eggs in a nest on the ground concealed only by vegetation.

It has two very small tufts of feathers from the top of its head giving it its name. It is often seen flying around hunting in daylight hours.

In northern wooded areas, especially in Manitoba, there is the great grey owl. It has a large round head, large facial discs and bright yellow eyes. It uses the nest of large birds such as a hawk or heron.

Much more common is the great horned owl. It has large feather tufts protruding from each side of its head resembling horns. It is capable of killing a full-grown turkey. Some that have been shot or found dead even had porcupine quills embedded in them.

In the winter, the white, arctic horned owls fly down from their northern habitat to hunt mice on the southern prairies. In their arctic home, they make their nests on the ground among the tundra vegetation.

Around my home, the population of eastern grey tree squirrels seems to be increasing. They can get into mischief and make a real mess in and around our towns. A partially grown one appeared on the roof of one of my bird feeders. It was a warm day so he stretched out flat on his belly like a dog and went to sleep for a good half hour.

I once quoted an article by Muriel Stewart about a pair of pigeons that built a nest out of nails on her balcony. In a second article, Stewart tells of another pair of pigeons on her balcony whose nest contained two eggs and was made of twigs and drinking straws in a secluded area.

She said it was two weeks before two wee birds appeared and the devoted parents were very busy indeed. The birds grew and became beautifully feathered. To her surprise one sunny afternoon she ventured out to find one pigeon backed into a corner alone.

For several days a very lonesome pigeon could be seen still in its nest corner. Then one morning she saw five pigeons perched on the balcony railing. The next day the same thing happened again. Now the lonely one seemed more venturesome as it went to the railing. Its head was very busy moving back and forth as it looked down.

Its next move was to go under the railing at the very edge of the balcony. Stewart saw her opportunity to make it fly so she gave a metal chair beside the bird a good whack. The startled bird took flight. That's one way to show a young bird it can fly.

S. Bergon of North Battleford, Saskatchewan, wrote to say that a Baltimore oriole used to nest every year in his shelterbelt but now he never sees it anymore.

It seems that there is a definite decline of songbirds. However I am pleased to say that in my area orioles are as plentiful as ever. Maybe next year they will return to your shelterbelt.

# Cats Like to Munch on Chipmunks

All summer a pair of chipmunks lived in our lilac hedge. We enjoyed their company and their antics. This morning when I stepped outside to go to the city, there was a cat that I had never seen before staring intently into the hedge. Chipmunks do not like cats, but cats like chipmunks because they make a tasty meal.

I yelled at the cat but, instead of running away, it disappeared into the jungle of lilac stems. I couldn't go away and leave it or the chipmunks would be gone for sure. I tried my best to scare the cat, yelling and prodding with a long stick. But it would only move from one end of the hedge to the other. I got a brain wave and got the water hose (cats hate water). I screwed on an attachment to eject water in a straight, forceful stream.

One shot of this and the cat was out of there in high gear. The only problem was it dashed across a clearing and up into a tree; it was still in the yard. A couple of shots of water hit it dead on, but it climbed higher. Another squirt of water, but the determined feline climbed even higher. At this point it became confused and let out some howls of anguish. My heart went out to it. I felt rotten that it was so frightened; it was a young cat and no doubt full of affection for humans, as most cats are.

Thank goodness at that point it climbed down the tree and dashed away for friendlier parts. Aside from being wet, it came to no harm and I felt solace in knowing that my chipmunks were spared for a little longer—perhaps for at least another season!

My picture today is of a big female yellow-shafted flicker posing at the entrance to its nest in a hollow stump. I found this particular stump a few years ago in a large grove of aspens. A flicker had excavated a nest inside the stump. I tapped the side with a stick to see if anything would fly out, and heard a loud buzzing sound inside. It was the voices of young flickers thinking that mother had just arrived with a beak full of food for them.

Hungry young flickers always make this loud buzzing sound, and one might think the stump was full of bees. The situation was an excellent chance for photographs, so I made a blind to hide in with the camera. I didn't have to wait too long before the mother flicker arrived and I got a few good shots.

Flickers are a species of woodpeckers. They get their name from their call, which sounds like a rapid "flick, flick, flick." The male and female look much alike, except the male has a black streak from the bill and under the eye referred to as a mustache.

Flickers are fond of ants and other ground insects, and so spend a lot of time on the ground. They are quite different from other species of woodpeckers who hunt for food largely in trees.

When I visited the stump again the following spring it had fallen over on the ground. This was an excellent chance to have a natural ready-made flicker house so I loaded it in the trunk of my car and brought it home. I fastened it to the fence in a secluded part of the yard and hoped a pair of flickers would nest in it. All summer long it remained empty.

Two more years came and went, and still it remained unused by flickers or anything else. This year I tied it up against the trunk of an elm tree about six feet above the ground and partially obscured by a white spruce tree.

A day or two later a pair of flickers suddenly appeared in the yard. Another day or two later I saw one land on the side of the log. It looked into the hole, then dropped down inside. They settled in and reared a family, but not before I got a few photos.

Incidentally flickers in the prairie provinces are yellow-shafted flickers—the underside of the wings and tail feathers are a golden yellow. In British Columbia there is a red-shafted flicker—the gold is replaced with salmon red. Both male and female yellow-shafted flickers have a dash of red across the back of the head, but this red does not appear on the nape of the red-shafted.

Where the range of the two meet, or overlap, hybrids may be seen, each showing characteristics of the other. Occasionally on the farm at Boggy Creek I used to see hybrids.

This flicker nested in a hollow stump.

Tiny, pencil-shaped crystals bend the sunlight to create sundogs.

# An Enchanting Winter Sky

What kinds of dogs don't bark? If it is cold and clear we can see them shining brightly in the sky on either side of the sun. They are sundogs.

To find out exactly what causes a sundog I consulted the book *Exploring the Sky by Day* by Terence Dickinson. As he explains it, the beautiful splashes of light called parhelions are commonly known as mock suns or sundogs. They appear only when the sun is very low in the sky. Cirrus or cirrostratus clouds must also be present because they are made of the right kind of crystals—six-sided and shaped like short pencils. The little ice pencils sometimes float straight up and down in the air. When they do, they refract or bend sunlight just the right way to cause sundogs. If the sundogs are especially bright, each will be colored red on the side closest to the sun, blue on the far edge and yellow in the middle.

Sundogs are brightest in the winter because the tiny pencil crystals are more common then. They can be seen at any season of the year.

I remember one cold day last year I saw the biggest and brightest sundogs ever—they were startling and beautiful. The bottom of the "dog" came down to almost touch the ground. Sometimes high around the sun and connected to each sundog there is a ring or halo. Although solar halos are quite common, they often go unnoticed because the sky is very bright whenever a halo is present.

These halos are made of ice crystals that refract sunlight at an angle and thereby create the ring effect. Sometimes a halo can be seen around the moon. My grandmother used to say a ring around the moon means it is going to rain, and in summer it very often did.

Every now and then someone will ask where frogs and toads spend the winter. Frogs, like turtles, burrow into the soft mud or ooze at the bottom of streams and lakes and in bogs and marshes. Toads dig into the soil, usually near a boulder or building or some protective cover.

Frogs and toads are hardy characters and regardless of winter weather always seem able and willing to serenade us when April and early May roll around.

At this point I might ask what creature can stick its tongue out without opening its mouth or parting its lips? A snake. This is due to a small groove at the front of the mouth.

# Each Bird Species Builds a Distinctive Nest

**The meadowlark builds her nest on the ground under a canopy of grass.**

Birds nests are fascinating to many of us. Part of the fascination, I suppose, is that almost every species makes a different kind of a nest and we, being of curious nature, are always thrilled to find a wild bird's nest with eggs.

It could be carefully hidden away in some secret place, such as out on the short grass prairie, in the woods at the base of some mossy tree trunk, under a log, up in the branches of a tree or down in a low clump of bushes. Each species has its own desire of where it will have its nest.

A meadowlark won't build its nest in a tree because it's a bird of wide-open prairie spaces where there are no trees; so naturally the nest is on the ground among the short grass. It, like other species, has its own particular style—so it is tucked in, so to speak, under a canopy of grass which the bird itself arranges. The eggs are white, blotched with brown.

The mourning dove usually makes a very flimsy nest in the lower branches of a tree. She is not averse to nesting on the ground. When she nests in a tree it is usually on a broad branch near the trunk. It is so sparse of material the eggs are in danger of falling out and often do if the bird flushes in a hurry. In that respect the nest on the ground is more stable.

Some species of warblers nest on the ground, while others choose a low bush. The yellow warbler makes a neat nest in lower shrubbery. It is made of fine dried grasses and lined with such soft material as plant down, deer hair or rabbit fur. Cowbirds make no nest of their own but will lay their eggs in smaller birds' nests and will often select the yellow warbler nest.

The yellow warbler doesn't always allow such rude intrusions. She isn't able to cast out the cowbirds' eggs, which are larger than her own, so she will simply go to work and build a new nest on top of the old one and try again. Sometimes she will try as often as four times.

Our American robin builds its nest in a tree crotch, on an evergreen bough, or on a ledge. Unlike the mourning dove's nest, the robin's nest is a sturdy one. The main cup of the nest is of mud but grass, rootlets and shreds of bark are lined within and vegetation may be on the outside as well. The robin's eggs are a beautiful blue.

The veery, a close relative of the robin, builds her nest on the ground, extremely well hidden among the vegetation at the base of a tree. Occasionally it will be located on a short stump in some secluded place. The nest is like a large doughnut cleverly woven of grass, inner bark shreds, moss, animal hair and plant down. The veery's eggs are blue, almost as blue as the robin's.

One of the most distinctive nests is that of the oriole. It is a woven bag of grass, plant fibres and other fine materials tied on and suspended from a slender branch high in a tree. By the way, they almost always use deciduous trees.

When the female incubates her eggs her weight slightly closes the nest sack at the top. Once after a severe wind and rain storm I found an oriole's nest on the ground. The branch to which it had been attached had broken off. It was a freshly made nest, and I couldn't help but notice the sweep-clean aroma of the grasses and other material.

The eggs of the oriole are white with scrawly marks.

The hummingbird, which so many people are interested in, builds a truly beautiful and fascinating nest. It's not much bigger around than a 50-cent piece. It is made of the most delicate of materials, such as pieces of lichen and moss, lined with the finest of plant down. The structure is saddled over a branch and cemented together and held with spider webs.

The two white eggs are about the size of peas.

The barn swallow chooses to nest in a sheltered spot out of the sun and rain, often inside an old deserted building or under the eaves. Her nest is made of mud, cup-shaped and lined with feathers.

The favorite place of the modern cliff swallow is under a bridge or sometimes under the eaves of buildings. Its nest is made of mud but is shaped like a bottle. Cliff swallows nest in colonies so many nests may be plastered together. In earlier times when there were no bridges or buildings, these swallows were obliged to plaster their nest on the face of cliffs.

Woodpeckers, as most people know, peck out nesting cavities in tree trunks. Usually the tree is in the dying stage, if not already dead, so the excavation work is easier than in a living tree. The white eggs are simply laid on a soft bed of sawdust.

One could go on and on to talk about this subject, for there are still many other species with interesting nesting habits, species such as crows, magpies, hawks, owls and all of the variety of marsh birds.

# Marshes Are Nature's Hideaway

A picture of a couple of water plants is featured here. They are arrow heads and horsetails. The arrow heads have the broad, arrow-shaped leaves. The horsetails are erect and fringy. Some kinds of horsetails grow in water, others on land.

I am not very knowledgeable regarding the identity of the various species of horsetails, but to make a hazardous guess I'd say the species here is either swamp horsetail, seeing that it is growing in the water, or common horsetail.

Regardless of the species, a habitat such as the one in the picture is ideal for many kinds of water wildlife. Frogs and snails will live and hide here, not to mention species of water bugs.

Little ducks can camouflage themselves in such ideal places. Muskrats feed on the tender shoots under the water. In other words, it's one of nature's hideaways.

Arrowheads have attractive flowers. There are three snow-white petals with yellow centers or stamens. Arrowheads grow from a bulb that the early Indians called a "wappatoo." Apparently they are good for human consumption and are reputed to have saved the lives of early settlers and Indians in times of food scarcity.

The yellow-bellied sapsucker is a species of woodpecker, but isn't too popular with growers of fruit trees or cut leaf birches. In the spring the sapsucker will make a pattern of holes on the trunk of these trees that will fill with sap. The sapsucker will then not only drink the sap, but also feed on the insects that are attracted to it.

The harm is that if the bird drills too many holes it could become harmful to the tree, and in some cases the tree might even die.

Aside from this, the sapsucker with his red forehead, red throat and yellowish breast is a beautiful and interesting bird. Sometimes it will allow very close human approach, while at other times it is quite wary. Here are two cases sent in by separate readers illustrating unusual close approaches. Ruth Dixon of Kenosee Lake, Saskatchewan, writes:

"Yesterday, another visitor put in his appearance—a yellow-bellied sapsucker. And if you please, he was helping himself to the syrup in one of my hummingbird feeders. I went out to take one of the feeders in to refill, and lo and behold if he didn't come and try to sit on it while I was holding it. Failing that, he decided to sit on top of my head. What a brave one."

Pat Fairbairin of Brandon, Manitoba, writes: "We saw this sapsucker sitting on a water tank on the golf course at Shilo, just a few miles east of Brandon, pecking at the tank for all he was worth. He sounded like 'Rosie the Riveter.' I walked up to it very slowly and upon reaching the tank I cupped my hand over him, then he flew away. I am sure it was a young bird as it appeared so fearless. Unfortunately, this was the last day we saw our musical feathered friend."

Pat asks why he would peck so determinedly. In answer to this—it wasn't really pecking, it was drumming. And it wouldn't be a young bird because young ones don't drum that early in the season. Most woodpeckers drum. The reason they do this in the spring is to attract a mate. Later in the season they drum to let other species of their kind know about their established territory.

Song birds sing to accomplish this same end, but woodpeckers can't sing, and so they drum out the message. Anything that proves to be a good sounding board might be used, such as the tank that you mention, a tin chimney, a loose piece of bark on a tree trunk or the tree trunk itself if it is partially dead. The drumming can start as early as late March when the mating season is starting to approach.

The common black-billed magpie is often frowned upon by many people. It is an attractive bird, but is reputed to be a nest robber and is said to cause wounds in cattle's backs when it pecks at their warble worm lumps or sores.

I have raised cattle for over 50 years and not once did I find any evidence of magpies attacking them in such a manner. I won't deny it hasn't been done elsewhere, but in my own opinion it is a rare occurrence.

Jean Bidinger of Caroline, Alberta, finds magpies a most interesting species. She writes: "Because I find the magpies so fascinating we started putting scraps of food out on the patio railing, and the parent birds came for them. However, instead of feeding all the scraps to the young, my husband and I observed them burying the scraps.

"Once the little magpies were out of the nest they sure kept parent birds busy, and we saw them taking the young (with the little short tails) to some of the hidden caches and watched the parent birds with their strong beaks dig out the food for the young. They soon learned to fend for themselves (while) hunting about for the hidden tidbits.

"Each morning there would be a magpie on the patio railing, and if it would find no food it would gently twitter until I took some to it. The bird would wait on a small shed until I went back into the house before he came for it. It was not uncommon to have several magpies at one time feeding together. They are experts at hiding food. A few mornings ago I observed an adult magpie burying something. After the bird had flown away, I went out to see what it was. It was three kernels of cat-food hidden in the grass."

Arrow heads and horsetails provide lots of cover for marsh dwellers.

# Curious Weasels Make Great Mousers

My illustration today features a curious weasel. I was driving down a back country road late in the fall. There were patches of snow in an otherwise bare pasture field. I was hoping I'd see a white weasel but never really expected to see one. Then to my surprise a piece of white ran out of a snowdrift and across a bare stretch.

Sure enough it was a long-tailed prairie weasel all dressed up in its pure white winter coat—except for a black tip on the end of its tail. I slipped a 300 mm lens on the camera and slowly walked to where I saw the weasel disappear down a gopher hole.

I crouched down about 18 feet away and waited. I figured it would live up to weasel-form and not stay down long. I was right. Five minutes later up popped his white head. I focused the camera while he studied me with beady black eyes. I never moved a muscle.

Weasels are curious, so he raised up a little for a better look at this strange human character. I still didn't move, so he moved up farther. He still didn't know what to make of it all so he bent his body in a comical way for a still better look. That is when I captured the pose.

After that he came fully out of the hole, stood up on his hind legs, stared at the camera for a second or two, and then took off across the flat to disappear down another hole.

This experience brought back memories of a weasel I saw a number of years ago in an almost identical situation, only when the other one went down the gopher hole it came up holding a mouse in its jaws. Weasels are great mousers and around grain bins should never be discouraged. They are also good ratters.

Going back still more years I remember riding a horse down a country road one day. At one place the road went down a steep hill. It was winter and the ditch was level with snow. I was puzzled to see a smallish black or dark object coming up the ditch towards me. As we drew closer I could see it was a dead rat being carried or partly dragged by a white weasel.

I am not sure where he got the rat, but there was a barn two or three hundred yards farther down at the bottom of the hill, so no doubt it was there.

I marvel at the strength of that weasel, for the rat would weigh as much as himself, I am sure.

Sig Jordheim of White Bear, Saskatchewan, wrote this interesting account about a goshawk. "Goshawks seem to be becoming more plentiful than usual in this area; perhaps they are attracted to this farm because of the shelter belts and bird feeding stations. I have seen as many as three at one time with almost daily harassment of the farm pigeon flock.

"One juvenile bird was persistent in making the farm yard his hunting ground and one day chased some bantams into a wire pen. I closed the door to the pen, captured the hawk and, after banding it, sprayed green paint on its tail and underparts. I put it in a cardboard box and drove it some 20 kilometres away and released it.

"The next day I did not see it. The second day a goshawk was pursuing pigeons, but being towards the rising sun I couldn't see the green paint. But the third day it came back and I recognized the marked bird. The fourth morning I noticed pigeons out early. This is a sign that something was in the cote, so on checking, here was the same goshawk inside the building. It had eaten one pigeon, killed three and wounded one more.

"The entrance holes for the pigeon cote are 4 by 5 inches and the hawk was 21 inches long and had a wing span of 40 inches, weighing one pound, 10 ounces. So it is twice the size of a pigeon. There is no perch in front of the entrance hole so the bird could not alight and force its way in. This shows the perseverance that is prevalent with these birds."

A curious weasel bends for a better look at the photographer.

The underwing moth roosts in the daytime
on some object that blends with its coloring.

# Underwing Moths Blend In

My picture today is of an underwing moth. There are more than 100 species of underwing moths in Canada and the United States. Usually several species, or kinds, can be found in one locality. By day they often roost in the shade on some object, such as a wall or a tree trunk, that blends with their coloring. Once the sun strikes them they will shift around to be in the shade again. Their color ranges from light to dark.

If the dark grey ones spend the day on the trunk of a tree, they blend so well with the bark they become almost invisible.

Some naturalists say the best way to collect them is at night, after painting tree trunks and stumps with a mixture of brown sugar or fermented fruit juice as bait.

Underwing moths get their name from the bright color of the underwing, which of course is not seen when the wings are closed.

The caterpillars of underwing moths feed on the leaves of poplar and willow, but little harm is done to the trees.

Mrs. R. Mawson of Ardmore, Alberta, has sent two color pictures of a pair of barn swallows perching on a wire. Nothing strange about that except one had a pure white head. She writes: "At first other swallows harassed her, but she was persistent and finally with the help of her mate, who was just an ordinary fellow, she built a nest and hatched out three ordinary young. After the young were flying all over the yard she built a new nest on a bend on our eavestrough. I was wondering if you or any of your readers have seen a swallow like this."

I would say that this swallow is a partial albino. That is to say there is a lack of normal color pigment in the feathers of the head. Sometimes complete albinism takes place in birds, mammals and humans. Partial albinism is common with English sparrows and evening grosbeaks, but this is the first time I have heard of it in barn swallows. I would say it would be a very attractive bird.

Ivy Sallee of Camrose, Alberta, wrote to tell of a friend who put out a line of tree swallow boxes that yielded 51 eggs producing 46 young, a good and worthwhile project. She also told of once nailing a flat-roof plastic birdhouse by her bedroom window. She said a sparrow built a nest in it, and at the same time a robin built a nest on top of it. Both hatched out young around the same time. She also had a robin build a nest in a tomato can that was half full of rusty nails.

Hello to Jessie Lowes of Coronation, Alberta, who sent pictures of young hawks in the nest taken by her grandson Dale and his friend Mark. I hope he keeps up his interest in nature photography. I sometimes think we don't look at the sky often enough to enjoy the beauty in the clouds. One of Dale's photographs showed them to be awesome and dramatic.

A fellow was here the other day who said he must have had a strange visitor in his flower bed sometime during the night. All the petunia blossoms on the outside of the bed had disappeared; they had been completely eaten off.

He also said that stalks of corn had been pulled down, their husks opened up and the corn nibbled off by very sharp teeth in a neat and clean manner.

I suggested he didn't have one creature in his yard that night, but two. The one with a fondness for petunia blossoms would be Prickly Porky, the porcupine. The mysterious fellow who tackled the corn patch would be a ring-tailed rascal known as the raccoon. They just love nice fresh corn on the cob the same as you or I do.

They say that crime does not pay. But, for that matter, neither does farming!

# How Do Gulls Find Food in the Snow?

One of the most common gulls to fly over the prairie lakes and marshes is the one featured here today, the ring-billed gull. This is a medium-sized gull, and the black ring that circles the mandibles near the tip make it easy to identify. Most farmers are familiar with the smaller Franklin's gull, as flocks of this species will often follow his implements up and down the field searching out grubs and bugs in the freshly cultivated soil.

It's not uncommon to see a few ring-bills intermixed with the Franklin's, but after picking up a few grubs or a mouse or two, they will gradually move on to other places.

Ring-bills are beginning to appear on the southern prairies. I have recorded them in late March. I remember one year on a day when it was snowing quite heavily I looked up to see two ring-billed gulls flying overhead. This was roughly around March 26. How gulls can find food in this country at such an early date I am not sure. Lakes are usually still frozen, but I suppose such fish as dogfish, left on the ice by winter anglers, would help out to a degree. Perhaps they would get a certain amount of energy from pecking at the snow, but when they are usually such hungry creatures, one wonders how this would be possible.

A lot of interesting letters have come in lately. In reply to a query about turtles in northern Saskatchewan, Mrs. John Lyall of Rossendale, Manitoba, wrote to tell of one her husband photographed at Caribou Lake in northeast Manitoba. This was doubtless a painted turtle. Apparently the species does range farther north than we realized.

A couple of years ago Lyall reported an albino barn swallow, and last year her son who lives at Pinawa (northeast of Winnipeg and next to the White Shell) saw an albino deer. Wouldn't that be something to see and photograph? One could refer to it as "the ghost of the forest."

Speaking of albinos, Mrs. L. Gibson of Drumheller, Alberta, says she saw a partial albino robin in her yard last fall and wonders how often these albino conditions occur.

Albinos are fairly common. At least that is the conclusion that I have arrived at by the numbers of readers who report them. This condition can occur with any species of animal, including people. It's due to the lack of color pigments in the hair, feathers or skin.

Thanks to Dorothy L. Wright of Lougheed, Alberta, for an interesting letter. She asks how swallows feed their young? The biggest part of a swallow's diet consists of flying insects. These are caught on the wing and simply shoved into the open mouths of the young. By the time young tree swallows are three parts grown, two or three will meet the food-carrying parent at the nest entrance with bills agape and chattering loudly. Into those mouths I've seen a mother stuff insects, the largest being a blue darner dragonfly.

Mrs. Marcel Van Steelandt of Deloraine, Manitoba, wrote to tell that she had a screech owl on January 13 of this year. It was roosting in the pole barn and is the first one that she and her husband had ever seen.

Thanks to John Chalmers of Boissevain, Manitoba, for writing and giving such a good report of the goings-on of wildlife in his area. He says that last summer was one of the best he has seen for wildflowers. In his unbroken land he had three species of gentians, and lady's slippers bloomed in abundance. He says it is remarkable where the lady's slippers came from, as until three years ago he hadn't seen one since 1929. But now they grow even in the most unlikely places.

Apparently much of Manitoba has had a good winter for birds. This is quite the reverse to the area where I live in southern Saskatchewan. Carol Badiou of Treherne, Manitoba, says she has blue jays, nuthatches, evening grosbeaks, chickadees, ten purple finches (males in gorgeous red), juncos, hoary redpolls and even eight or nine goldfinches. All feed at her place each day. I am wondering if the goldfinches might possibly be pine siskins, for in winter they certainly do resemble female goldfinches. But then again with birds anything can happen.

Carol is also a butterfly hunter and has identified 44 species. She says the forest tent caterpillar outbreaks in the last three years have resulted in a huge population of parasitic flies, and she blames them for decline in that area of the large silk moth numbers. It is to be hoped nature rights this balance.

The ring-billed gull occasionally stops by a farm to snag a few grubs, bugs and mice.

# Hawks and Kestrels Take to the Air

Drive out into the country in August and you are almost bound to see big hawks on the power poles and fence lines. If they are large and look chocolate brown with rusty red underparts, they are juvenile Swainson's hawks. These juveniles have different coloring from the adults.

There are red-tailed hawks too, but there seems to be more young Swainson's in evidence than red-tailed. Juvenile red-tails are almost white below with dark mottling across the abdomen. They are about the same size as the Swainson's.

Sometimes we see flocks of sparrow hawks or kestrels. They are beautiful little hawks. Although they are called hawks, they are really falcons and have the falcon's notched or toothed bill.

The strong black and white face markings and large amount of red on the back and tail identify the kestrel. The name sparrow hawk leaves the impression they prey on sparrows. That is not the case; they are so named because of their small size. Grasshopper hawks might be a more appropriate label because they destroy a large number of these harmful insects.

Once when I was driving down a back road several kestrels were on the fence post and overhead power lines. I was paying attention to these and never saw the one on the ground; it flushed directly in front of the car. I saw it too late and it was killed instantly. I stopped and picked it up. What a beautiful thing it was! So beautifully made and marked. We don't realize just how beautiful many of our wild creatures are until we actually examine them closely.

There are lots of interesting things to see at this time of year—not only animal life but also plant life. The plant in my picture, tufted fleabane, may still be found in certain areas. It's a pretty thing that is found out on the dry prairies. A standard 50 mm lens was used to make this photograph.

I have had some very interesting letters lately and I might say now how much letters from readers are appreciated. Without letters this column could never have lasted as long as it has.

John Cook of Birch Hills, Saskatchewan, wrote of an interesting incident. "My brother-in-law witnessed an unusual occurrence. When straightening up their garage, a red squirrel ran out of a tarp they intended to fold. The squirrel dashed around in such a frenzy they believed it wanted to escape, but refused to leave when they opened the door. Upon lifting the canvas, a small, pink, hairless animal rolled out, which they identified as a very young squirrel.

"As soon as the humans withdrew, the mother raced over to the tiny infant. Using her front paws like hands, she proceeded to place the little animal's head on its belly and rolled it up into a ball. Opening her mouth very wide, she pushed the rolled-up infant into her mouth and carried it out the door and to another building across the yard.

"The squirrel repeated this procedure until the young were all moved. Even then she returned to repeat the chattering fuss, which made the people believe she was incapable of counting."

Mary McGillivray of Salmon Arm, British Columbia, asked: "In your years of bird watching have you ever seen coots display? Three or four males will turn heads out and lie along the water, rear ends raised, black tails fanned and showing startling black patches almost the size of the black tail.

"This pose is held for several minutes; then they swim off normally, and suddenly as if on cue, back they will go to repeat it again.

"It's a fascinating sight and I have asked a few oldtime bird people about it and no one had seen this performance. Would any of your readers have seen this odd display?"

I might explain that coots are black, chicken-like birds that, from a distance, look like black ducks swimming. They are very common on our prairie sloughs and marshes. Their display takes place during the spring mating season.

Evelyn Dickie of Drumheller, Alberta, wrote: "The sapsuckers announced their arrival last spring in a very annoying way, and the neighbors as well as myself lost a few hours of early morning sleep over their antics for at least two weeks after their arrival. One would fly on to our TV antenna or aluminum chimney and tap for a few minutes at a time about 4:30 a.m. each morning and continually throughout the day. Could this tapping on a non-insect object have anything to do with their mating ritual or could it be that they were sounding out their territory to other birds?"

You are right on both thoughts. Sapsuckers and other woodpeckers are not gifted with song, and so this is their method of calling out for a mate and also to announce that this particular area is their territory.

The ruffed grouse is not blessed with song either, and so he drums out his message from a favorite log by whipping his wings back and forth. Strange indeed and most interesting are the ways of nature.

**Fleabane prefers the hot, dry, sunny prairie.**

# Autumn Leaves Drop and Winter Birds Return

Before taking its winter nap, the chokecherry shows off its autumn color.

My picture today is of chokecherry leaves in autumn color. Thinking back over the years, at this date the foliage of some tree species will be gone. Much depends on whether it has been dry. If it has been, the trees usually lose their leaves earlier than under good moisture conditions.

Frost also plays an important part if it comes early. Green ash is the first to turn in the fall and the last to get leaves in the spring. Manitoba maple, or box elder, doesn't give that much of a color display and leaves tend to shrivel up quite fast. Elms retain their leaves sometimes into

October if they are frost-free. The poplars and willows retain their leaves and are about the last to turn color and eventually fall to the ground.

The smaller species of bushes and trees give lasting color. Gooseberry leaves are orange-red and red osier dogwood are deep maroon, which contrasts nicely with their pearly white berry clusters.

While the trees and bushes of the prairies turn color and fade, the trees in parts of Canada with milder climates stay green much longer. Coastal and southern parts of British Columbia are good examples, as are Ontario and the Maritimes.

Lots of birds species are long gone for southern climates, though there are still lots around to make things interesting. Our winter species will soon be arriving, so autumn is a good time to start thinking about getting feeding stations established. Baskets or lumps of suet suspended from tree limbs and sunflower seeds mixed with canary seed satisfy many bird species.

Chickadees will dine on sunflower seeds in the shell, but they really go for those that are shelled. These usually have to be bought at a grocery store. Of course, the shelled seeds are more expensive, so unless you are a millionaire don't feed them to evening grosbeaks, as they will eat you out of house and home.

Winter bird feeders are a great source of enjoyment, as you never know just what kind of bird may appear unexpectedly. Marjorie E. Webb of Speers, Saskatchewan, certainly enjoys her feeder. She said that one day last February a stranger suddenly appeared at her feeder. The bird's feathers were so puffed up against the bitter cold that its shape was disguised, but it was at least as large as a blue jay, though with a very short tail, not at all like the jay's long one.

The overall color was a dark brown, breast and back alike, with some darker patterns not easy to see.

We all know that on rare occasions wild ducks will crossbreed with one of another kind; but who ever heard of a goose mating with a duck? Blanche Barnett of Edmonton has. She writes as follows: "The Cowichan River flows by my sister-in-law Frances Neilson's home. Last year two pair of ducks mated and made their nest close to her house. She started feeding them, and they soon came right up to her door demanding service.

"One of the drakes disappeared last fall. The remaining pair mated this spring, and the female laid one clutch of eggs, but a hungry raccoon stole them all. At about this time her mate met with misfortune, and she was left alone."

Frances was looking out of her window one day in early May, and to her astonishment there was a Canada gander mating with her friend the duck. After several matings she made a nest.

The gander was fierce in his protection of his lady love. He attacked anything in the immediate territory and finally had the river cleared of all other bird species for a good half-mile.

Frances and a nature-loving friend determined that the raccoon was not going to have this bunch of eggs. So Frances, at great peril of injury from Daddy Goose, ran out and collected each egg as soon as it was laid.

When the duck was finished, she had 11 off-white eggs. These were put in an incubator to hatch. They were due to hatch about the middle of June, but alas not one of them brought forth life.

This is a very unusual thing to happen. But the eggs didn't hatch because there was just too much difference between the genes of the duck and the goose. I guess this is something that Mother Nature simply doesn't allow.

# Squirrels Scamper on the Highwire

**The grey squirrel uses its long, bushy tail for balance when scampering through the tree tops.**

I was walking down the street after getting the mail one day recently, and as I approached a power pole I saw a flash of movement at the top of it. As I drew closer there was no movement that I could see.

I came around to the opposite side and looked up. I wasn't really surprised to see a bushy-tailed grey squirrel pushed as flat as he possibly could against the pole. I couldn't help but chuckle to myself because it looked so cute. But it did surprise me when quick as a flash it reversed positions—instead of facing up it was facing straight down and in this position seemed as equally at home as it was before.

I stood and watched it for a minute or so, which probably embarrassed the squirrel, knowing that he was discovered. At that point he decided to leave, not by coming down to the ground, but by nimbly scampering along the insulated wire to the other side of the road and then leaping into the branches of a clump of trees and out of sight.

When it comes to tightrope walking these squirrels are professionals—what balance and body control they have!

Grey squirrels, now inhabiting parts of Saskatchewan and Manitoba, are originally imports from southern Ontario. They have also been introduced to British Columbia and are especially common in Stanley Park in Vancouver. They have three color phases: grey, black and reddish brown. But the most common color is grey or black. Any squirrels that I have seen in Stanley Park have always been black.

The fox squirrel looks much like the grey squirrel but is slightly larger. It is making its way into Saskatchewan in greater numbers, and it also has three color phases: black, beige-grey and red. But most here are beige-grey. Their underparts are tawny in color compared to the white of the grey squirrel. The grey squirrel has a white eye ring and its paws are light brown. The fox squirrel has ochre-colored ears, cheeks and feet.

Grey squirrels are active all winter long, as are the fox squirrel and the little red squirrel, except during a severe cold spell. Then they stay curled up in their dens, which are usually located in a cavity in a trunk of a tree. This could be a large woodpecker hole or natural cavity, and if it is large enough several will snuggle up together.

In summer, when the animals don't need as much protection from cold and storms, they may make a nest of grass, leaves and twigs up in the branches of a tree. These nests look like crows' nests but they are skillfully made and will shed rain.

Like all species of squirrels, the grey squirrel loves nuts. In fact my picture today shows a grey who had just polished off a walnut that was placed on a board for him. I used my 70–120 mm zoom lens in this particular case and the film was Kodachrome 64.

If there are no nuts or acorns about, they can very easily exist on other kinds of food items such as berries, tree buds and seeds. In summer they even go for grasshoppers. Birds' eggs are also a relished treat. Some people with kind hearts will put out food for them. Peanuts and sunflower seeds will do just fine. Red squirrels will also benefit from the same type of fare.

I think the most attractive part of a grey squirrel is that big, bushy tail. Some declare that they sit in the shadow of their tail on a hot day to keep cool. I doubt this is true because a squirrel never sits still long enough to reap any benefit of such a habit. But it does help the squirrel to keep its balance while traversing on the slender branches or running along a wire as I described.

As far as I can find out, mating takes place around the end of January, with a gestation period of 44 days. An average lifespan is estimated to be six years, but captive ones may double that, the main reason being they would live a protected life with no predators and lots of food.

Less Barr of Cut Knife, Saskatchewan, said that every year waxwings come and strip his mountain ash tree absolutely bare. Apparently his tree is the European mountain ash variety and is the only tree in town that seems to interest them. The flavor must really appeal to them because the other kinds which have small clusters are left till later on in the winter.

# Wild Geese Adore a Blueberry Patch

Blueberries—what lovely, sweet delicious fruit! Unfortunately, they don't grow in many southern areas of the prairies. Up in the northern parts of the country, in the open areas of pine woodlands, is where they like to grow best.

They are great to eat with cream and sugar, great in pies and great in many other ways. Birds eat them too, as they enjoy most wild berries. But blueberries are a favorite. Northern people tell of how wild geese will really invade large patches of blueberries and clean up every last one of the juicy fruit. Maybe this is where the expression "loose as a goose" originated, and one can understand why.

On certain fruit farms a cultivated species of blueberry is grown for commercial use. The berries are larger and good, but haven't quite got the flavor of the wild kind. For those not familiar with blueberry growth, I might explain it is a low shrub from 12 to 24 inches high. The flowers are greenish white, about ¼ inch long, and grow in small clusters.

If you live out in the country, or in a cabin in the woods, you never know what may come down your chimney besides Santa Claus. It might be a raccoon or it might be a squirrel or even a bird, as Hilma Maus of Menisino, Manitoba, describes in a recent letter.

"I had an unusual experience recently. I live alone in a country home. I still have my wood cook stove in my kitchen. I had been away overnight and when I came home at noon the next day I set about to light a fire in the stove. There was some noise in the stove pipe so I did some checking, but found nothing," she wrote.

"Later I lit the fire again. I heard nothing more until I decided to make a fire in the stove the next morning. This time there was great rustling in the pipe as the fire began to burn and smoke came out of the stove. The pipe damper was now turned to close. I opened the damper and the fire burned well.

"Now I set about to see what was in the chimney. I have a two-storey house and a wood furnace in the basement. There had been no fire there for some time. I removed the pipe from the furnace, and with the use of a mirror and a flashlight, I checked the chimney both up and down. At the bottom of the chimney, at the clean-out hole, sat a bird.

"He managed to fly out the pipe hole where I had removed the pipe to the furnace. It was a duck—it had webbed feet and a duck bill. I caught him as he flew against the wall and fell behind some firewood.

"I offered him a drink of water, but he wouldn't drink. Then when I opened the door and set him down he flew away at great speed. He had been in the chimney for over 24 hours so I was glad he could fly so well."

Hilma lives in southeast Manitoba near the Minnesota border. A lot of that area is forest reserve, so under those circumstances I would say the bird was either a golden-eyed duck or a wood duck, as these species nest in hollow trees and stumps. The duck doubtless investigated the chimney for nesting possibilities and slipped down inside where it couldn't get out.

William Ryan of Candle Lake, Saskatchewan, was a reserve officer in that area for 30 years and has had plenty of opportunity to observe wildlife and other forms of nature. In forested country like Candle Lake, Bill says there are some species of wasps that grow really big.

He tells of entering an old unused building and seeing hundreds of bulldogs (a large species of fly) on the windowpane and one big wasp. At first he was going to kill the wasp but then watched in amazement as the wasp would attack and kill a bulldog, instantly snapping the head right off. Bill says it reminded him of a weasel in a hen house.

Frances Emro of Kipling, Saskatchewan, describes a bird about the size of a bluebird, but yellow with darker brown wings. The yellow extends down the back and is paler underneath.

I am not 100 percent sure, but it sounds to me as if it could be a female oriole.

Commercial blueberries can't match the flavor of the wild berries, which flourish in northern pine woodlands.

This red-breasted nuthatch works from the top down, traveling head-first in its search for insects and their eggs.

# Nuthatches Can Be Comical Winter Guests

Does anyone have red-breasted nuthatches? Sometimes these tiny creepers stay all winter. They usually nest in the boreal forest farther north, but nuthatches begin to show up in some southern places in August, when the greatest bulk of the species starts moving southward.

In September if they find a good feeding station, where suet and sunflower seeds are supplied, they just might decide to linger on into the winter.

Nuthatches are most attractive and interesting in their acrobatic actions. They seem more at home traveling upside-down on tree trunks than they do right-side-up. Their odd, cute little "quanck" calls are really woodsy sounds, and at times they seem almost as confiding towards humans as the chickadees are. You can identify a red-breasted nuthatch by its rusty red breast, the white line over its eye and its greyish blue back.

Doreen Pearce, who lives right in Sherwood Park, Alberta, says she had two red-breasted nuthatches at her feeder all last winter. In early November of this year she again had red-breasted nuthatches at her feeder and has high hopes of them being her winter guests. She also remarked that evening grosbeaks were there feeding on her Mayday tree berries early in the season.

Following is a story about a grouse from Parley Bagley of Twin Butte, Alberta:

"One evening in British Columbia I was driving down a shady lane in an old pickup truck. I stopped at my neighbor's mail box to deliver his mail. With the motor idling, I stopped to read the newspaper headlines. The truck had a burnt exhaust valve and gave out an odd muffled splutter, not unlike a drumming grouse.

"Suddenly out of the woods came a male grouse. He flew up to the pickup at hood level in an angry flutter and hovered there a moment in somewhat of a surprise. Finally he settled to the ground and determinedly kept looking for his challenger. Sidling all around the truck, he centred on the battered and leaking muffler.

"Strutting and sparring, wattles as red as a frustrated tom turkey, he tried to do battle. Laughing at his antics I kneeled beside the truck and egged him on. After a few skirmishes he gave up and sneaked off into the brush with a baffled look over his shoulder.

"My neighbor, Bill Torrence, was working in the woods nearby. When he heard my motor idling he came out, thinking to get his mail. He found me at the mail box, still chuckling about the baffled grouse. He asked if I was getting bushed or perhaps there was something funny in the newspaper. When I told him about the grouse he didn't believe me. It had never happened to him. When I showed him the tracks in the dust under the truck, he reared back his head in wonder."

Such a thing occurs far more often than we realize. A few years ago I had a letter from a chap who worked his land with an old two-cylinder John Deere tractor. He said that on this certain spring day every time he went "putt-putt" by a certain grove of trees, a ruffed grouse would come out with spread wings, race across the intervening space and attack the front wheels of the tractor. Apparently the "putt-putt" of a John Deere sounded to him like a challenging grouse.

Another time here at Regina Beach my friend Alex Bryden was building a house in a grove of trees. When he would start to hammer at a certain time of day on one side of the house, a ruffed grouse would fly out of the trees, land on a mound of earth beside the house and start drumming like crazy.

# Skinning a Porcupine Is Hard Work

**A porcupine has stripped the outer layer of bark from these branches, preferring instead the delicious inner bark.**

So far this winter I have seen very few winter birds in my part of the woods. There have been no flocks of Bohemian waxwings, grosbeaks or even snow buntings.

Yesterday, however, when I stopped at the house next door, I found a dead frozen Bohemian waxwing in the snow. I had not seen or even heard any waxwings, although I had been outside a good part of the day.

Apparently it hit the window, killing itself instantly. I picked it up and marveled. I have seen many waxwings over the years but this one was indeed a beauty. Not a feather was disturbed and its plumage was smooth as silk. No other bird has a feather arrangement of such smooth satin texture. Its color is beautiful, the tail tip yellow gold, the under-tail coverts rich chestnut, continuing around the eyes and merging into the black mask. On the wing are snow-white markings and the small red "droplets" that give the waxwing its name. (They look like small drops of sealing wax.) We don't realize the beauty of these wild creatures until we actually hold them in our hands.

In one column my feature picture was a porcupine snuggled into its den in the side of a bank. In an earlier column, the photograph was of a den in the base of the trunk of a big balsam tree. Any kind of a hollow or cavity satisfies Mr. Porky as long as he is concealed and not likely to be disturbed. Even a thick brush pile that he can crawl under will serve the purpose.

In winter porcupines climb into the branches of trees and gnaw off the bark, particularly the inner bark, which is rich in food value. Today's picture shows many branches denuded of bark by a porcupine. As long as this animal stays out in the woodlands he is fine, but if he gets into a fruit orchard or somebody's prized evergreen he can do a lot of harm and decrease his popularity with humans.

I have seen porcupines climb up into a tree in winter and stay there all day and all night. Willow trees are a special favorite. The animals should be free of headaches, for the bark possesses a chemical called salicin, which is related to the substance present in today's Aspirin. Native people years ago discovered that chewing inner willow bark eased their aches and pains.

A porcupine's track in fresh snow is not hard to recognize. It is a sort of waddling track with footprints quite close together. If the snow is deep the animal's side hair touches on each side of the track, leaving a mark, and there is also a mark from his dragging tail.

Years ago when I was young and foolish, I tried to skin a porcupine a friend had shot. Why I wanted to do this I am not exactly sure. Porcupine meat is said to be good to eat, tasting much like pork, but I am sure I had no intention of eating it. What a job it was to skin; the hide was so fat and greasy. The tail was the hardest part of all, like a mass of tough sinew attached to the skin.

The tail is the porcupine's secret weapon. When attacked he simply rolls up in a ball. If anything gets too near he gives it a slap in the face, the quills stick in and there they stay. My advice to people who see a porcupine for the first time is don't touch it; just look.

Someone wrote to ask if the northern shrike is a common bird on the prairies. I used to see one or two every winter, but never more than that.

The northern shrike is a hardy character. It doesn't migrate as far south as its close relative, the common shrike. Its summer breeding grounds are much farther north, near the tree line from Alaska to Labrador. The bird is also found in Eurasia and Northern Africa.

The northern shrike is like the common shrike in shape and flight pattern, but larger and darker, with a lot of black and white on the wings and tail, a black mask around the eyes and a delicate barring on the breast. It has a very pleasant winter song, although few people have had the privilege of hearing it.

Shrikes have hawk-like habits. They have toothed beaks like little hawks, but their feet are only good for perching and are not strong or taloned. They hunt small birds, mice and grasshoppers in summer, and birds such as redpolls and house sparrows in winter. Fortunately, there is an overabundance of the latter species.

When a shrike captures its prey it impales it on a thorn, the barb of a fence, a small broken tree branch or any other sharp object. It is then in a position to tear its prey apart with its beak.

# Colors Camouflage the Marbled Godwit

My photo today features a marbled godwit standing at the edge of a prairie slough. Its long legs and long bill allow it to search for food under the water as well as on land. It wades out into five or six inches of water, then, with its long, slightly upturned beak, prods the soft mud to find water bugs, worms and snails. Godwits also dine on land insects such as grasshoppers. Since they don't eat grain, they are helpful to farmers.

These big, sandy-brown waders have long been my favorite shore birds. They are noisy as well as picturesque. Their loud calls of Korect! Korect! Korect! can be heard near almost any prairie slough.

One year, after an April snowstorm, I drove to the highway for the mail. As I came over the hill I was surprised to see three or four big marbled godwits in the middle of the road. Standing with them, in the snow by the side of the road, were a half-dozen Wilson's snipes. I had no idea that these species had already arrived on their spring migration. They all flew away immediately, of course.

Snipes have long bills too, but not as long as godwits', which measure close to five inches. Marbled godwits nest near sloughs or small lakes, in small depressions sparsely lined with bits and pieces of grass.

The brooding bird sits so quietly, passersby can walk right past and

**The marbled godwit helps farmers by eating grasshoppers, not grain.**

not see her. She flattens herself out over the eggs, her head and long bill pressed to the ground, her colors camouflaging her perfectly. Her instincts not to leave the nest are so strong that I once squatted down within two feet of a nest, and the female bird never batted an eyelid. There are even records of a female godwit allowing herself to be gently stroked as she sat on the nest. But, like other birds, godwits are unpredictable. On another occasion, the same bird that allowed me to squat beside her flew off the nest in great alarm when I was 20 feet from her. She flew around my head shouting her loud Eradica! Eradica! call.

When first hatched, godwit chicks are covered with down. They are mottled brown and fawn in color and have a relatively short bill. As the chick grows, so does the bill.

Jerry Iverson of Meota, Saskatchewan, observed an unusual feeding habit in a flock of Canada geese. He wrote: "While living at our cabin in the Cree Lake area of northern Saskatchewan I noticed within walking distance of the cabin there is a large burn of about seven years ago. The new growth of young pine is one to two feet in height. There are thousands of these burnt areas.

"While picking blueberries one afternoon (September 10, 1987) I observed there were many goose droppings everywhere in this berry patch and no blueberries. We have found evidence around the lake shores of geese walking into the burns, but I never thought they would fly out to feed on blueberries like they do into farmland farther south in the fall."

Geese are intelligent creatures, and I imagine it wouldn't take them long to discover there is good eating in berry patches.

A reader who lives near Saskatoon wrote to say that on Sunday, March 8, he and his wife and four neighbors saw a pure white adult fox looking for food along a hedge south of their farm buildings. He has seen red and black foxes, but never before a pure white one.

In the north there are white foxes, called Arctic foxes, but none live as far south as Saskatoon. The fox they saw must be an albino red. It no doubt has pink eyes.

Nearly 100,000 species of insects live in North America.

# Insects Are Integral to Nature's Scheme

As I sit down to write it is still very hot, about 38°F. The air over the lake is a blue haze; it's the smoke from the forest fires up north carried down by a northeast wind. Those fires are devastating, but the smoke down here has a rather sweet aroma. The open prairie is very dry. The wind blows and reblows; it adds to the dryness. Hang a shirt or a towel out on the line and it dries immediately.

Thank goodness for our lake. It provides a refreshing coolness if you are a bather. With little fresh water going into it and with the warm weather, many people are concerned it will become green with algae. Blue algae is dangerous for both the domesticated stock and wildlife if they drink it.

My picture today shows a group of beetles on a head of thistle. Just what kind of beetle they are I am not at all sure. I've never seen them before and I've never seen them since. Looking through the *Audubon Society Field Guide to Insects of North America*, the beetle that resembles them most closely is the goldsmith beetle, but its range doesn't cover western Canada.

Insects are ugly, yet their colors can be beautiful. They have their place in nature. Some are beneficial to man; others cause crop losses and damage to tree foliage. The beneficial species pollinate our flowers and fertilize the soil. Bees make honey and some moths make silk. Mosquitoes and black flies make life miserable for humans as well as animals.

It is said nearly 100,000 species of insects live in North America. The study of insects can be most interesting, especially so in such species as butterflies and moths. Photographing them can be a real challenge. Closeup attachments to the camera are necessary because of their small size. In today's picture I even used a flash so I could use a small lens opening to give a better depth of focus.

Over the years I have often received letters from someone who cared and looked after an injured bird, and the injured one has become a regular family pet. Back in April 1983, I wrote about a mourning dove that had become a pet of Josephine Gibson of Regina, Saskatchewan, who has written to me again.

"We call our dove Fluffy, and she was seven years old last spring. She cannot fly very much due to her age. She laid two sets of eggs every year for five years. This past two years she did not lay any eggs.

"She has the freedom of the home by day but insists on sleeping in the bird cage at night. We have attempted to set her free, but she doesn't want to fly away; she always comes back. Her longest absence was four hours one summer.

"Perhaps she knows her wing will never be strong enough for a flight south. The reason we call her Fluffy is she constantly wants to sit on our shoulder as we watch television or read the newspaper. Then she fluffs out her feathers, relaxes and makes a purring noise to let us know she is happy. She then falls asleep. She is indeed a very wonderful pet.

"Then another story this spring. A young robin sat in our pine tree and sang. My husband looks after our daughter's four spitz dogs, and when they wander too far, he whistles to call them home. This robin imitated the human whistle and now incorporates this whistle in his song. We recorded the whistle on tape that this intelligent robin has mastered.

"Our back yard is a very busy bird sanctuary. We have four sets of purple martins, one set of tree swallows, several sets of robins and Baltimore orioles using the string I put out for them to build their nests. We buy twine and cut it ten to twelve inches long. We separate the strands and lay them on the tree branches. This is ideal nesting material for the orioles.

"In one day our yard is visited by as many as 10 different species of birds. It's a wonderful place to live, next to a park, if you are bird lover."

Yes, Mrs. Gibson, I fully agree. To get lots of birds and other wildlife there is nothing like living in a treed area.

# Masked Raccoons Rob at Night

**Although raccoons cause damage on farms, they are attractive and intelligent.**

A long time ago I read a poem, at least I think it was a poem, about the month of November. I can only remember the first line, "November woods are bare and still." Nothing is more true because the woods in my part of the country certainly are bare, and quiet too!

You can walk in them and there is not a sound. I did the other day, but then I discovered if you did stay long enough, and listened hard enough, you probably would hear the cheerful "dee, dee" notes of a chickadee giving you a welcome.

Then, as you listened, you might have picked up the tapping sound of a downy woodpecker pecking at some food discovered in a crevice in the bark of a tree. From a distance you might have heard the gentle nasal call from a red-breasted nuthatch. These are the three species you are most likely to hear in my district. In your area, if you have other species of trees, it may be different.

My picture today features a raccoon that I photographed one night on my picnic table. It was about 10 p.m. We were quietly watching television when we heard a loud thump on the deck outside. We quickly turned on the deck light and saw a raccoon shaking the sunflower seeds out of the bird feeder. We got another surprise, because on top of the picnic table was another raccoon with his head in a pail of sunflower seeds that I had put there for safekeeping.

A lot of people, especially farmers, do not like raccoons because of the damage they do around grain bins and elsewhere, but they are very attractive and intelligent. These two looked cute with their black masks; they looked like the little burglars they were at that moment.

I dashed for the camera, but the raccoons, already nervous about finding themselves revealed in the bright light, quickly made a getaway over the rail of the deck.

I thought if I put the lights out they might be back, so I replaced the pail of seeds on the picnic table with the dog dish with dog food in it. The camera and flash were ready.

Things went along quietly for about 20 minutes, when once again there were noises on the deck. This time we didn't turn on the light, but peering out through the window we could make out their dark forms—one at the feeder and the other on the picnic table. I quietly opened the door, just enough, aimed the camera at the dark object and fired the flash! The result is today's illustration. Yes, the raccoons disappeared very fast, and as far as I know they never came back. Not yet anyway.

A while ago I gave a report of a mourning dove owned by Mrs. Josephine Gibson of Regina, Saskatchewan. She named the dove Fluffy and she has had it for numerous years. It has been a perfect pet in her household. A letter from her recently revealed that the dove now has a new companion but not a dove.

"Following my recent letter to you on the mourning dove, Fluffy, we had a very heart-warming experience. One evening as we were visiting relatives on their sun deck, out of the blue a baby budgie came and sat on my husband's shoulder. So we captured him and took him home. We named him Muffin, then tried to find the owner. But no results.

"I put the budgie in the cage with Fluffy at night—that's the only time Fluffy is in the cage, otherwise she has the run of our bedroom.

They became instant friends. It is so heart-warming to see these two different species of birds so loving and gentle to one another. They sleep side by side, and follow one another in flight around the room. They even eat together and preen one another.

"It's so cute and delightful to see the budgie preening the dove's head; the dove sits there with its eyes closed enjoying the entire procedure.

"Fluffy has not laid eggs for two years, but did lay eggs after the budgie came to live here."

Yes, Mrs. Gibson, that is a very unusual thing for two species of birds to become such close friends. Thank you for sharing this experience with us.

# BC Honors the Insatiable Jay

My picture today features a blue jay with a peanut in its beak. Every morning they would come for their peanut breakfast before the sun was up. In fact, it would be barely light enough to see.

To get pictures at that early hour I had to use flash to get an exposure. With Kodachrome 64, slow shutter speeds or time exposure were out of the question, as the birds were far too active. They would fly in, land, grab a peanut and be gone again. I used a 70–210 Pentax zoom lens about seven feet away from their landing spot.

I see in a Vancouver newspaper that the Steller's jay has been chosen as an emblem of British Columbia. The writer, Tony Eberts, describes the Steller's jay as "an intelligent but mischievous bird that sometimes steals food from campgrounds." It beat out seven other birds including the varied thrush, peregrine falcon and trumpeter swan in a provincewide vote that drew 80,000 ballots.

The jay, when legislation is passed, will share emblematic duties with the dogwood blossom, as provincial flower, and British Columbia jade, as the provincial gem. Late last year the western red cedar was designated as British Columbia's official tree.

Manitoba's bird emblem is the great grey owl; Saskatchewan's is the sharp-tailed grouse and Alberta's is the great horned owl. The Alberta tree emblem is the lodgepole pine. It would be nice if Manitoba and Saskatchewan had tree emblems too.

The prairie provinces have wildflower emblems: the rose for Alberta, the wild prairie crocus for Manitoba and the western red lily for Saskatchewan.

The Steller's jay is common in British Columbia. It is also numerous in the Rocky Mountains of Alberta but rare in Saskatchewan. There were two sightings for that province a long time ago, and the birds were a long way from their natural range. One was seen at Indian Head in 1923 and a pair was sighted in Yorkton back in the 1920s and a single bird in 1944. I would love it if one would surprise me at my feeder one day.

The blue color of the Steller's jay is not as brilliant as our eastern blue jay. It is much darker and has a smoky black front and head. The habits of both Steller's and blue jays are almost identical.

A friend of mine recently returned from the Toronto area of Ontario. He said at the place where he was staying there was a feeder that was patronized not only by blue jays, but by beautiful red cardinals.

Thomas A. Harper of Simpson, Saskatchewan, wrote that he has enjoyed my nature articles for many years, especially the last one about those insatiable blue jays. "I have been involved in feeding them since I moved into my valley in 1920 and have enjoyed their antics through the years," he said.

"What I use for them is a slab of frozen suet; most locker plants will give that away now. In earlier years when farm butchering was common suet came from that source. Durum wheat is another food of theirs and is much cheaper than those peanuts you mentioned. If you offer them a choice of durum and red spring wheat, they leave the milling wheat and stuff their pouches with the durum and leave the other wheat for the sparrows.

"Usually I cleared a bare spot in an open area of the yard where the farm cats couldn't sneak up on them. But this winter I saw them sneaking food out of the dishes I feed my cats in, and that's not recommended in my yard. So I placed a plastic pail on a six-foot metal post, filled it with durum, stuck a piece of suet in it and placed the feeder five feet from my living room window.

"Now I can enjoy watching them carrying the wheat away and sometimes some suet, but that is mostly used by the chickadees and woodpeckers. Some days there are three jays feeding and transporting the grain to store in orioles' nests, or in the snow by tree roots, or behind loose bark or any other spot that suits them.

"Every year I plant sunflowers in the flower garden by the house, and they spend the early fall cleaning those up. As of now there are seven of them carrying the wheat. And it starts as soon as it is light enough in the morning and goes on all day."

That is a good tip about feeding the jays durum wheat. Wheat isn't worth much these days so you may as well let the jays have it.

This blue jay has grabbed a peanut from a window feeder, but jays also eat suet and durum wheat.

The only duck with curled tail feathers is the mallard drake.

# Mallard Drakes' Spring Plumage Is Majestic

My picture today shows a mallard drake relaxing and preening itself in the shallow water of a prairie slough. A 400 mm lens was used to take the picture. I was concealed in a blind some 20 feet away.

The duck was absolutely unaware that a human being was anywhere near at all. That's the advantage of shooting pictures, or simply observing wildlife, from a blind. You see them doing their own natural activities. They are not alert, not nervous—just perfectly natural.

Ducks and shore birds, when gathered into groups, are so often talking to each other. At least it seems that way. They make little peeping sounds or chirps and, in the case of the ducks, little muttery quacking sounds. So in a way they are not too unlike people.

It's pretty hard to beat the spring plumage of a mallard drake—the vivid green head and neck set off by a white ring at the base separating the green from the chestnut breast.

When I was a young lad I was quite fascinated by the curled black feathers of the tail. The mallard drake is the only duck that sports curled tail feathers.

Mallard drakes have pale yellow beaks and bright orange feet and legs. Once, years ago when I was hunting ducks, I shot a mallard drake that had only one leg. The other was taken off at the first joint, but perfectly healed over. What the cause of this was would be interesting to know.

It could be that as a duckling a fish, a pike most likely, tried to capture it and bit off a leg. Young ducklings have been captured and eaten by large pike.

Then again the missing leg may have been taken off by a muskrat or a mink trap in the water. I once knew a trapper who set his trap in shallow water for mink. On the pan of the trap he had fastened a shiny piece of round tin. His theory was that mink are curious little animals, and upon seeing the shiny object, they would come to investigate and get caught. On checking his trap one day, however, he found captured not a mink, but a mallard drake by the bill.

The duck, too, apparently was curious when it saw the shiny object and gave it a poke with its bill, probably to flip it over to see what was underneath, and this of course was a sad and fatal mistake. The trapper felt bad himself and never tried that method again.

Mallard ducks as a rule build their nests on the ground in some secluded and sheltered place such as in tall vegetation or low bushes. Sometimes, rather surprisingly, they will choose a high place off the ground such as in a deserted crow's nest. This is always a surprise.

Once, in a clump of diamond willow (this species of diamond willow usually grows in thick clumps), I discovered a crow nesting in high branches and about five feet below it, in an old crow's nest, was a mallard duck.

Crows, as almost everyone knows, are not at all averse to eating duck eggs. I am not sure if the crow ever ate the duck eggs because I did not return to that place for some time, and when I did both nests were deserted.

Mallards have also nested in split tree trunks as high as 20 feet above the ground. Then of course the question is asked: how do the little ones get down? They simply jump. Being light, they flutter like leaves to the ground, bounding off branches to break the fall.

All female mallards are dressed in sombre colors for the purpose of camouflage when the bird is setting on the nest.

Sometimes mallards will nest very close to farm buildings in a habitat that is prowled by cats and dogs. I remember one time on the farm sitting by the kitchen window and looking out to see a mother mallard parading proudly across the lawn with a group of newly hatched young trailing behind. I couldn't believe my eyes.

Old Rusty, the dog, was curled up in the grass only a few feet away. His eyes were closed and he was, apparently, asleep. I held my breath, hoping and praying some instinct wouldn't waken him. If it did it would be goodbye little ducks.

But mother mallard did make it away safely. Where in the yard she nested I never did find out. I must have walked past her while she incubated her eggs. This is where camouflaging colors come in; she sat tight and her nest was never revealed.

Along about July the beautiful color of the mallard drake gradually fades. This is their molting period. Even the flight feathers of the wings fall out and for some time they are flightless. As fall approaches, and the new feathers come in, their brilliant colors gradually return.

# Lady's Slippers Are Unique and Dainty

Many lady's slippers are rare, so resist the urge to pick them.

At the time of writing where I live the country is dry. We took a drive to Calgary and it was bone dry all the way there—even Banff National Park appeared dry.

Trees have turned a beautiful green in sharp contrast with the brown grass of the hillsides. Amongst the trees there are a few flowering wild plants, such as Canada violets, but others out in the open spaces will have a tough time. The meadow where I photographed the three short-stemmed lady's slippers won't produce much this year unless it suddenly gets abundant rainfall.

Lady's slippers are fascinating plants, unique because they are so different from other wildflowers. They are shaped like little moccasins. I suppose because they are so dainty they have been called lady's slippers.

There is another kind of the yellow variety, larger than the short-stemmed, and it is simply called the large yellow lady's slipper. The flowers are more than 1¼ inches long and are greenish yellow with purple spots and streaks. Both kinds are found in moist wet meadows and poplar woodlands.

In the wooded area of the more northern parts, there are more varieties of lady's slippers. There are stemless lady's slippers that are pink and about two to 2½ inches long. The common habitat are bogs and moist open shades of the forest. They are classed as rare, so if you find one, resist the temptation to pick it.

There is another, very rare to Saskatchewan, known as sparrow's egg lady's slipper or Franklin's lady slipper. It is almost pure white and its habitat includes damp, cool, sandy areas in northern forests.

One of my favorites is the exotic Venus slipper. It too is very rare and has a fairy-landish quality. It is delicate and beautiful, and is also called Calypso for the Greek goddess of that name. Its favorite habitat is open evergreen woods, particularly under the pines.

All these lady's slippers are members of the orchid family. Other orchids grow in the timbered areas of the prairie provinces. The most common ones are the coralroots. Really fascinating plants are found in the northern woodlands and in the forests of Cypress Hills.

John Cook of Birch Hills, Saskatchewan, often writes to this column. Last winter he spent some time in Mesa, Arizona, where he has a winter home. He wrote: "One of the many fascinations of that area was watching the roadrunners. Living as they do, in a heavily populated area, they become accustomed to people, which makes it easier to observe them at close range. Roadrunners are efficient flyers, but prefer to move very quickly on their strong legs. They usually keep shrubbery or a similar barrier between themselves and any observer, which makes it difficult to photograph them.

"Last year, I had an opportunity to watch their courting ritual. The male bird offers nesting material to the female; by accepting his offering she indicates her acceptance of him as a mate."

Cook said the nest made of sticks and grass was in a bush beside the patio of a mobile home, about six feet off the ground. She laid five white eggs about 1¼ inches long. Before leaving for Canada Cook checked the nest and found only four eggs.

Cook also said he has an uncle who lives in Salmon Arm, British Columbia, who used to be a hydro lineman. He was often called to help the wildlife people erect washtubs atop tall trees to attract Canada geese.

Mary Jo Burles of Cawley, Alberta, wrote that this spring she had Canada geese nest 40 feet up in an old tree by the river.

# Thirsty Chipmunks Enjoy the Bird Bath

The nesting duties for most robins are finished by the end of July. My picture shows an American robin at her nest. The eggs had hatched and the young looked naked and helpless. Indeed they are, for often they become easy victims for magpies or crows.

I took the picture by remote control using a standard lens and flash. The camera was placed on a support very close to the nest, and when the bird appeared at the proper place at the proper time the camera was set off by remote control. I used flash to fill in the dark contrasting shadows.

Robins who nest far away from farm buildings or in remote forest regions have a far better chance of having their young survive than those who nest in cities or towns. The young often jump out of the nest before they can fly properly and easily become victims for cats, dogs or curious young human beings. Each year in June I get phone calls from people who say they have discovered a young robin on their lawn who can't fly, or some child has brought one to them. They ask me what to do with it.

Unless they want to raise it themselves (and they never do), what else can they do but set it up on a branch of a nearby tree and hope the mother robin will hear its cries and feed it for another day or two until it can fend for itself. I wonder if the chances for the young robin's survival are very great.

But looking on the brighter side in the world of nature, some charming things can often be observed. For instance, I have long been familiar with chipmunks, but I never thought of them needing a drink of water. They are so often seen in places where there is no water that I figured they manufactured their own water from the food they ate, the same as ground squirrels who live out on the arid prairie.

This spring I placed a large crockery plant dish on a short block of pine and filled it with water to make a bird bath. Two chipmunks lived in the hedge nearby, and for them I put out a small dish containing sunflower seeds.

The attractive little creatures appreciated this handout very much, which didn't surprise me. But I was surprised when I saw one climb up the pine block to the dish filled with water, perch on the edge of it, then lean down to the water and take a long drink, lapping up the water in the same manner as a dog. Now they do it every day and several times a day.

Here is an interesting letter from Mrs. M. M. Mutch of Penticton, British Columbia. She writes: "We live in what we refer to as the outskirts of town. Having decided against cats many years ago, the bird population has grown in multitudes, consisting of not only migratory birds but also quail and pheasants, which we feed all year round.

"One summer we noticed a female quail that appeared to be having difficulty walking due to excessive weight, or perhaps I should say size. My husband noticed daily that she was getting larger, and finally one day she was so large her body covered her feet and she could no longer move about.

"My husband was able to walk over to her and pick her up. On investigation we noticed that her feathers and skin seemed to balloon out from her body. He brought her to the house and after further prodding and probing we agreed that her skin had somehow detached from the flesh and an air pocket had built up between the two.

"We laid her on her back on the kitchen counter and I cradled her and held her down as my husband disinfected a sharp knife. We parted her feathers and my husband made a small slit in her breast. Immediately the air could be heard escaping.

"We pressed her feathers to her body to squeeze out all the excess air and her body returned to normal in minutes. By this time she was fighting to get up. We held her gently to insure that she would be all right and, so we could keep watch on her, we spray-painted her tail feathers red. We returned her to the area of her mate and the two of them rejoined one another excitedly.

"We watched her for several weeks until the red paint disappeared and we were no longer able to distinguish her among the many pairs of quails that resided in and around our acreage. To this day we do not know what caused the ballooning, nor have we ever seen it happen again. But we feel in some small way that we were able to save one little quail and insure that nature does carry on."

This is indeed a very strange case and I have no idea what would cause it. I wonder if it could be the result of a bump or a bruise.

Hazel Paton of Oxbow, Saskatchewan, says she has a northern oriole that comes to her feeder and dines on sunflower and millet seeds. Birds sometimes pull the darnedest surprises.

**American robin babies are naked and helpless, and often fall victim to magpies or crows.**

# Common Sora Rails Are Seldom Seen

When a sora rail senses danger, it usually just tiptoes away.

My illustration this week is a photo of an immature sora rail, which I photographed along the shores of Last Mountain Lake with my 300 mm lens. This is a marsh bird, quite common around wet, grassy shorelines of sloughs and lakes, yet seldom seen by the casual observer. One might hear sora rails calling and wonder about the "noise."

It is a fairly loud, long series of notes in a descending scale—not musical, but attractive to the ear of the naturalist. Some people describe the call as a maniacal laugh.

As I mentioned, the bird shown here is immature; the mature plumage is much brighter with more colorful patterns. The legs are greener and the short, stout bill is yellow. The first time I ever saw a sora it reminded me of some kind of small chicken parading around through the grass. Rails are skulkers; if you are walking through the marsh and a rail hears you coming it doesn't, as a rule, reveal itself by getting up and flying away. It simply steals away quietly into a thicker area of vegetation. If it does fly, it has a loose, dangling flight and only goes a short way before dropping down into the grass again. They are, however, strong flyers in migration.

You will note by looking at the picture the bird has long toes. These were designed to aid the bird in walking over vegetation in watery places; it's not so liable to sink in.

As a youngster I used to hear the expression "skinny as a rail" and I wondered if it had anything to do with this species of bird. It does seem to be able to contract, making its body slimmer to ease it in travelling through thick rushes and other close growth. But I am sure now that the expression is really referring to the rail of a fence.

The nest of the sora rail is a mat of vegetation attached to reeds or rushes a few inches over water. The eggs are tan with red flecks scattered throughout.

# A Fly Can Be a Thing of Beauty

There are many different kinds of flies. We have houseflies, horseflies, deerflies, fruitflies and blackflies, to mention a few. I am not quite sure as to the proper identity of the species in my picture today. But I call it a flowerfly. I see it only in the fall, and it seems to really enjoy flowers, especially the cultivated kinds.

In this picture the fly is investigating a marigold, which serves as an excellent setting to show the insect to its best advantage.

For readers interested in photography, I used a short-barrelled 100 mm lens coupled with bellows, and as I wanted to use a small lens opening, such as F16, to give a good depth of field, I used flash even though it was a sunny day. The bellows-and-lens combination allows a very close focus.

Insects are a definite part of nature and are beautiful, but in quite a different way. (Note those glossy and delicately made wings.) They are not the easiest things in the world to photograph, but it's a challenge and a lot of fun.

A while ago I used a report of a barred owl coming down a chimney and into the living room of a private home. Well, here is another interesting story sent in by Myrtle G. Moorehouse of

Aneroid, Saskatchewan, only this time it's barn swallows.

She writes: "We lived in a two-storey house. The window was quite high up, so I just left it open a couple of inches all summer. Occasionally I heard birds twittering quite loudly, but assumed they were outside. Then one morning a young bird started flying around quite frantic to get out. After a merry chase I caught it and gently took it downstairs and let it out. The next day another was flying around, and it was a repeat performance.

"When on the third morning another one appeared we closed the window; yet a fourth bird arrived on the scene. We couldn't imagine how it got in! Shortly after I removed the side curtains to wash them and I found a nest was glued to the wall, made of tiny mud pieces and dried grass. Was I ever surprised to find that that bird and her young ones had been living with us all that time and we never even knew it!"

Yes, Mrs. Moorehouse, I guess you were.

Hazel Paton of Oxbow, Saskatchewan, had goldfinches at a feeding shelf this summer and early fall. She says she fed them the smaller black sunflower seeds. She said she also had goldfinch at her feeder last winter. Carol Badiou of Treherne, Manitoba, reported goldfinches in winter also. At the time I felt they must have been pine siskins, another kind of finch resembling the goldfinch in autumn plumage. But then another letter came in from Ruth Dixon of Carlyle, Saskatchewan; she said that last winter was the first that she had goldfinches at her feeder in winter. She said she counted as many as 20 at one time at the feeding shelf. She described them as amiable as a chickadee slipping in and out of the feeder with no quarreling. This is a contrast to the evening grosbeak, who are pushing and shoving almost constantly.

It used to be you never heard of goldfinches spending the winter on the prairies, but now apparently they are. Cedar waxwings in winter were unheard of a few years ago, but now they are often seen. This illustrates how the pattern of wildlife is changing.

In summer the male goldfinch is bright yellow with black wings. Females are more olive with bits of yellow. Males in winter would resemble females.

There is a tremendous amount of wildlife being killed on the highways these days. Every time I drive I see evidence of this, and the longer the drive the more I see. Skunks, porcupines, ground squirrels and rabbits seem to be the most common victims, and outside of the ground squirrels, most kills happen at night. Skunks and porkies move slowly and car headlights confuse them. They have no idea of the monster behind the headlights or of its speed.

Jackrabbits get trapped in the beam of light. To them straight up the road is illuminated, but to each side is a black wall into which they are hesitant to run. Some motorists will slow down till the animal gets off the road, but others do not. Deer often get hit by cars, and I understand that in forested areas, especially in British Columbia, many moose die from car injuries.

I remember one winter day while driving to Regina unusually large flocks of snow buntings were on the highway, apparently after the grit in the gravel at the edge of the black top. I was amazed at the number of dead ones sprinkled along the highway. If people would only slow down while driving by such flocks many of the kills could be avoided.

This kind of fly loves flowers and appears only in autumn.

The thirteen-lined ground squirrel lives in wide-open, grassy areas.

# Striped Squirrels Disappear in Grass

Don't call me chipmunk and don't call me gopher—call me thirteen-lined ground squirrel. Chipmunks have nine lines down their backs while the thirteen-lined ground squirrel has exactly that, 13 lines.

Chipmunks love bushy treed areas, whereas the other one likes wide-open grassy areas. The lines and colors give excellent camouflage in their sun-dappled habitat. They are not related to the gopher.

We call Richardson's ground squirrels gophers, but they are not gophers. The true gopher on the prairies is the pocket gopher, which makes those mounds of earth we call mole hills.

The thirteen-lined is related to the Franklin's ground squirrel, which is much larger, more grey and has no stripes down its back. It can be found in treed and bushy areas. Both species have a long, trilling, bird-like, musical whistle.

Both species have long periods of hibernation. They go to bed early but get up at a respectable time in the spring. Like all ground squirrels they store food in their burrows for eating in the spring before other food is available.

The number of young varies from five to as many as 13. When out feeding in the grass, their colors protect them but they are constantly on the alert for hawks, foxes and coyotes.

At this time of year there is much new growth and trees are bursting into life. One of my favorite trees has been the trembling aspen, one of the most common aspens in Canada. It belongs to the poplar family and might be known as asp, quaking asp, aspen poplar, white poplar, popple, or smooth bark poplar.

The name trembling poplar is derived from the unique quivering or trembling action of the leaves when stirred by the slightest breeze. Trembling aspen is one of the first trees to leaf out in the spring.

It is at this stage that I think the leaves are at their height of beauty—so fresh and well shaped and such a pretty shade of green. Later, as the leaves become older, they become much darker.

Trembling aspen is not a large tree, averaging about 40 feet tall and eight to 10 inches in diameter. Under ideal conditions, some specimens have reached a height of 90 feet and a diameter of two feet. Most aspens that grow in prairie valleys are quite slender. They are sweet and fragrant with a smooth, whitish green bark.

They are also a favorite tree with many species of wildlife. Birds of prey, such as hawks, owls and eagles, build nests in their branches. Woodpeckers use the soft wood for nesting cavities in their trunks, especially after the tree is dead. Porcupines enjoy the buds and the tender bark of the branches.

Aspen is a great favorite with the beaver, not only for food but for dam-building material. Humans over the years have used the wood for firewood, pulp wood, veneer, lumber, box wood and matches. Like all poplars, trembling aspen reproduces quickly and easily by means of root suckers. It is one of the first trees to grow after a forest fire.

It is interesting to stop and consider the different shapes, sizes and locations of birds' nests.

The floating nest of an eared grebe is completely surrounded by water and appears to have little support from other growing plants. The main purpose of floating nests is security in case of rising water after heavy rains when the nest simply floats like a raft. From my observation, this is good insurance if the flooding is not too severe. But I have also seen colonies wiped out after a deluge.

# Fireweed Flourishes Far and Wide

**Fireweed is also called willow herb, because its leaves resemble those of the willow tree.**

My picture today features a nice stand of fireweed, the floral emblem of Yukon Territory and a worthy flower at that. The stout stems have a stock of many individual red flowers, and each flower in itself is beautiful.

The plant gets its name from the fact that it is one of the first plants to grow and bloom again after a forest fire. Of course, it doesn't bloom only where there has been a fire; it grows along roadsides and fields in parkland country where it is uncultivated. In fact, I have found a single stem of fireweed growing in a marsh-type habitat.

The late botanist and writer A.C. Budd wrote: "This is one of the most ubiquitous of plants being found over most of the northern hemisphere from east to west in America and from sea level to the higher altitudes. It is a good source of honey and it is fairly palatable to livestock, the upper and more tender tips being eaten."

Another name for fireweed is willow herb, because the shape of its leaves resemble that of the willow tree. Budd lists in his *Plants of the Prairies*, six subspecies, some taller, some shorter, and all with leaf variations and shades of flower color. The tiny, down-tufted seeds travel for miles on a summer breeze.

A reader from Yorkton, who doesn't want her name mentioned, wrote describing a very handsome wading bird she saw this summer at the edge of a large slough. Its body was about the size of a pigeon and possessed much black and white color. The rather longish neck and head was a pinkish fawn color. The bill was quite long, slender and curved upward. The legs, quite long, were bluish.

From this description it couldn't be anything but an avocet. These birds, along with godwits, curlews, and willets, are the largest of the wading birds, excluding members of the heron family, which are not really classed as waders, although they do wade.

Like the other three mentioned waders, avocets nest near water but on the ground.

Last spring I had the pleasure of watching four or five avocets feed in the shallow water in the Valeport Marsh at the south end of Last Mountain Lake, Saskatchewan. It was a beautiful sunny morning and what a lovely sight they made; a background of fresh green marsh grass with their images reflecting in the sky-blue water.

The avocet's method of feeding is quite interesting to watch. Instead of pecking down into the water like the willet and godwit, they sweep their bills back and forth in the water, thus catching any small water insect that their feet stirred up in the mud below.

The southward migration of avocets starts in August, and by the end of the month there may not be too many left.

August is the month when I hear the soft "yank, yank" call of the red-breasted nuthatch. They rarely nest in my vicinity of Last Mountain Lake, so when I hear them at this time of year I regard them as migrants.

Hazel Paton of Oxbow, Saskatchewan, has really been enjoying the birds that came to visit this year. According to a recent letter she especially enjoyed the waxwings and writes as follows regarding one pair:

"Today, June 26th, is a wild, windy, damp day and the waxwings are in a nest-building mood. So they have been coming to sit on my flower bed fence. They were picking up fragments of dried grass, fuzz and probably some dog hair out of cracks in the cement. Then one tried to ravel threads out of the cover of the old wedge foam cushion on one chair. I put out some bits of white cotton batting and they have taken some of that.

"They came right to the doormat at the screen door while I was standing holding it so the little dog wouldn't rush at them. They are so pretty.

"In spite of this wind I don't think it has wrecked any nests. One western kingbird has a nest in a bushy maple and she is getting well rocked. We must have five or six pairs of westerns this year—their nests are everywhere. One robin has a nest on the track for the big sliding doors of the Quonset. The doors don't interfere, but she is in the hot sun if it gets hot." (And it certainly did.)

# Grouse Scratch for Food in Tough Winters

My picture today is a close-up of a sharp-tailed grouse. I've nicknamed it the V for victory bird because its front feather pattern is a beautiful arrangement of Vs. Back in wartime, Winston Churchill of Great Britain would hold up two fingers spread apart to make a V, his sign for victory.

At this time of year sharp-tailed grouse can be found in the parklands, where they find shelter from the cold winds and trees to perch in on bright, sunny days. To get out of the storms at night they simply snuggle down in the deep, soft snow, which sometimes drifts over them. More than once I have been startled out of my wits when a grouse burst out of the snow at my very feet.

Food is always a problem during a long, cold winter. Tree buds, wild fruit and berries become important. If there is not much snow in the stubble fields, one may see a flock out there searching for grain. It is amazing how our native grouse can survive a tough winter.

Back in my farming days we often made oat sheaf stacks in a field close to the house. During one winter I noticed a few sharp-tails on top of the stack each morning and a few on the ground at the base of the stacks picking up oats that spilled out of the sheaves.

I got a small pail of wheat and scattered it around at the base of the stacks for the grouse. They found it fast and appreciated it. Each morning they would arrive just at sunrise for breakfast, so it became a daily practice.

It was an excellent chance for pictures, but at that time I had no such thing as a telephoto lens, so I figured if I lured them in close to the house I could get some shots from the window with a standard lens or even rig up a remote control device for an outside camera that could be clicked off from inside the house. Gradually I spread the grain closer and closer to the house until I had it only a few feet away and the grouse were beneath my very nose.

The flock grew from about 10 birds to 22. They seemed to time themselves by the rising of the sun, and as the winter progressed the birds arrived earlier.

What a pleasant sight it was to see them flying from the creek low over the field. With wings beating to slow down their progress they would land a few feet away from where I stood inside the house. As spring approached and the snow melted the flock grew smaller, until finally none came at all. The mating and nesting season was at hand.

When winter came again the following year I wondered if my sharpies would return. One morning I looked out the window and saw several sharp-tails in the exact place where I had fed them the previous winter. There was no grain and they were looking toward the house as if to say, "Aren't you going to feed us?" I wasted no time getting grain out and the next morning they were back again. For the second winter in a row I had sharp-tailed grouse for guests each morning.

I got pictures of them to mark the event. Today's picture wasn't taken there, but on their dancing ground several miles away. I took it from a blind using a 400 mm lens.

William Kinaschuk of Chase, British Columbia, sent in these notes on hummingbirds. "I feed ruby-throated hummingbirds," he wrote. "They arrive approximately April 15 of each year. I get over 200 to 300 each season and I use over 40 feeders which have two feeding holes each and have red caps and perches.

"I have found the best feeding mix is five to one. That is five cups of water to one cup of sugar. I make my own feeders from soya sauce and vodka bottles. I have found that no red color is required. I go through two or three gallons for over three months. It is necessary to wash out the feeders and holes about three times a week.

"Boil the mix (sugar and water) for five minutes and cool before filling the bottles. Do not feed honey. After a few hot days honey will ferment and will kill your beautiful hummingbirds. Too sweet a mix will also kill them. I strongly advise you to use good spring water if possible. Your house tap water may be very dangerous since it could contain rust, chlorine and other harmful ingredients."

Kathy Roth of Goodsoil, Saskatchewan, wrote to say she has a robin around her yard that was apparently left behind when its brothers and sisters migrated last fall. She wonders if it will survive.

Robins are pretty tough characters, and it is not unusual for them to winter in our cold climate. I have often seen them in the middle of the winter on the farm and also here in Regina Beach. Once I went for a hike around the creek on the farm on a very cold day in February. When I came around a bend I found a flock of seven robins perched on the lower branches on a clump of diamond willow.

The sharp-tailed grouse makes sure his feathers are clean and in place.

Identification bands don't harm the necks of whistling swans.

# Whistling Swans Pass through the Prairies

This is the time of the year (April) when the big white whistling swans pass through the prairie provinces on their way to their northern nesting grounds in Alaska and the Canadian low Arctic. The flocks we see on our open sloughs and lakes most likely spent the winter along the Atlantic coasts of United States from Maryland to North Carolina.

I read an interesting article once, probably in the *National Geographic*, about biologists who were doing a winter study of whistling swans in Maryland. Many of the swans were captured and marked by placing long plastic bands on their necks. On each band was a number large enough to read with binoculars from a good distance.

I might mention here, for the benefit of readers who may feel the bands may have an adverse effect on the neck of the birds, that the bands are very light and cause the swans no discomfort when feeding or otherwise.

One member of the banding team had a favorite swan. Whether it was larger and more magnificent than the others I am not sure, but it was marked clearly with a certain number. When the swans took off in the spring on their northern migration, the biologists followed by plane to do a study of the whistling swan in its northern environment regarding nesting and summer activities.

The member of the team who banded the favorite swan in Maryland got the thrill of his life when he found the same swan on a remote lake in Alaska! It was recognized, of course, by the number of the band on its neck.

Each spring when swans are seen on our sloughs and lakes, I get letters from readers inquiring what they are. Some people think they are whooping cranes and some call them trumpeter swans. The trumpeter is larger than the whistling swan and is rarely seen in Manitoba and Saskatchewan, although a few trumpeters do nest in the Cypress Hills of Saskatchewan.

The population of the trumpeter swan is not large at any time. Its numbers are greater mainly in British Columbia and the Grande Prairie region of Alberta. In winter they have become quite famous for their appearance at Lonesome Lake, British Columbia, and have often been filmed for documentary programs.

As I have so often said, one of the best photographic blinds is the ordinary motor vehicle known as the car. To photograph these whistling swans I simply drove down a back road along this particular slough where they were resting. Before getting to the place where I wanted to take my pictures, another car came from the opposite direction traveling at a dust-raising speed. The driver couldn't help but see the swans. But the beauty of the scene meant nothing to him, for he roared past them and me with stones and gravel flying in all directions.

I thought for sure the swans would fly, but to my surprise and delight the only indication of alarm they showed was to stretch their long necks in a listening attitude as if to say, "What was that?" So I progressed onward at a slow speed and managed several good shots from the car window using my 300 mm lens.

With high-powered lenses it is best to use a tripod, but that is most awkward from inside a car. So what I use is a small plastic or cloth bag filled with beans. (Don't look puzzled.) What you do with the bean bag is you lower the car window to the desired height, then place the bean bag over the edge of the glass. Work the bag down so that an even number of beans fit on either side of the glass and you have a perfect pad to rest your lens on. You can hold it very steady this way. Last summer I got a dandy picture of a moose using only 1⁄10 of a second shutter speed. This was because the sky was very cloudy and sprinkling rain, and the moose was in deep bush shade so the light was very poor. The picture came out sharp and clear.

# Pussywillows Herald Spring

**Diamond willow catkins start out as pussywillows before bursting into flower.**

For most of us, the pussywillow is the best symbol of spring. What we call pussywillows are really catkins of the willow tree. When they first come out of the bud they are soft and furry like a kitten. A few warm days later the catkins burst into flower, the yellow stamens laden with pollen. After that they become a mass of fuzzy seeds that blow off in the wind to land somewhere else and eventually grow more willow trees.

Nine kinds of willows grow on the farming and ranching areas of the prairies, and some have larger catkins than others. The catkins in my photo are of the diamond willow variety.

Now that we have entered spring, things in nature begin coming to life. Hibernating mammals start to wake up and stick their noses out of their burrows to sniff the spring air. How sweet it must smell after long months in a hole. Horned larks are now being flushed from the roadside in sizeable flocks, and tree sparrows are quietly and secretly hopping around in hedgerows and bushy areas.

I have received two letters with excellent skunk stories, one from Mary-Jo Burles of Pincher Creek, Alberta, and the other from Alvin Haight of Hanley, Saskatchewan. Here is part of Mary-Jo's letter: "Three years ago we had a mother skunk named Falina, who paraded her five little ones across the yard and up on the steps every day for a month to eat the cat's food.

"They were so tame she would come up and sniff at my toes as I sat on the lawn swing. But one night when we were in Calgary until midnight, someone didn't quite shut the back door and she brought all her babies into the house. Our 15-year-old grandson, Billy, who was in a wheelchair and in the house alone, heard something rummaging in the garbage can in the kitchen and left the TV long enough to investigate.

"Our black and white cat was up on the table but there were numerous other black and white furry things roaming around the room. 'I very quietly wheeled back into the living room and sat motionless,' he told us when we got home. 'One of the little ones came up and nosed around my wheels and I could see two under the dining-room table and still could hear some in the kitchen, so I don't know for sure how many were in the house, but I think they were all six.'

"I checked the whole house before we went to bed, and it was none the worse for the invasion. The only time Falina, the mother, threatened us was when the cat didn't want to let her and her family have all the food. I had a dollar bet with one of my daughters that I could have at least one of them eating out of my hand by fall. I won."

Here is Alvin Haight's story: "Back in 1923 we moved a granary and a mother skunk ran out leaving a family of four little skunks, perhaps only a day or two old. We had a cat in the barn with newborn kittens so we killed the kittens, with the exception of one, and put the little skunks with the mother cat.

"To our surprise she nursed them as her own, and they were about two weeks old before they had their eyes open. Soon they were running around the barn and drinking milk with the cats.

"It wasn't long before they were in the house and were great pets. They were friendly with the dog. In the fall we made a box home for them, where they stayed for the winter, but in the spring they took to the fields."

Edgar Danridge of Birtle, Manitoba, says he has enjoyed Prairie Wildlife for many years. He sent us a snap of a young skunk nursing on a contented cat. On March 24 last year, a skunk came wandering into his yard with a face full of porcupine quills. He has never heard of this before. I haven't, either.

# The Northern Oriole's Origin

Someone remarked the other day that to see an oriole flying through the trees was like seeing a piece of orange flame that got away from his campfire. I have often thought the same thing.

Most people will identify the bird in my picture hanging onto the wire of my hummingbird feeder as a Baltimore oriole. It could also be called a northern oriole. A few years ago it was most unusual to see an oriole drinking nectar from a hummingbird feeder—now it is quite common.

I think more people are putting out hummingbird feeders than in previous years, and so the orioles caught onto a good thing. Last summer I noticed that it was the female oriole that came to the feeder first; the gorgeous male appeared to be more reluctant. I believe he was browbeaten, for during the course of the day the female oriole would make 10 trips to his one.

As summer started to wane the female suddenly ceased to come at all and disappeared from the scene. I assumed she had left on her migration south.

For several days after her departure the male started coming almost steadily all day long. When he finally left he must have been tanked to the gills. With all that sugar water in his system he should have had enough energy to make it to Mexico in double time.

Interbreeding in the prairie provinces of the Baltimore oriole and

Bullock's oriole results in giving us what is called a northern oriole. Bullock's oriole tends to haunt the more southern parts of the prairies and the Baltimore, more the northern parts. Bullock's oriole has an orange stripe over the eyes and under the neck and cheeks. Also it has more white on the wings.

Hazel Paton of Oxbow, Saskatchewan, reports that for the last two years in a row, orchard orioles have nested at her place. The male of this species hasn't the brilliant color of the two previous ones; its brightest colors are deep chestnut.

All orioles build the same type of nest—a hanging bag of woven grass and fibres. I once made the statement that orioles only use deciduous trees to hang their nests in, but a sharp reader promptly informed me that I was wrong. She had one that hung its nest from the branch of an evergreen.

Orioles belong to the blackbird family. I am sure everyone has seen a blackbird harassing a hawk that might come too close to blackbird territory. Apparently the oriole has a trace of its relatives' protective instincts because Marion Parker of Buena Vista, Saskatchewan, observed two male orioles harassing a hawk last spring.

Lew and Dorothy Morgan of Marsden, Saskatchewan, wrote to tell of an unusual bird they had in their yard this past spring. It was a blackbird with a white head and shoulders and white on its legs also. This is the fourth summer they have seen a bird of this description but each year it appears to have more white on it. They wonder if it is the same bird getting whiter as it gets older. It nested on the ground across the road from their house for three years, but this year it nested in a Scotch pine in front of the house. At the time of writing it was sitting on the eggs so they did not see it quite as often.

It appears to me that this bird is a partial albino and is probably either a female Brewer's blackbird or a female red-winged blackbird. There is also a possibility that it was a grackle. But then grackles aren't really ground nesters. This albino condition is common with many different bird species but judging by the letters I get, I would say it is most common with English sparrows and evening grosbeaks. Why, I do not know.

Mrs. R. Gilroy of Oxbow, Saskatchewan, wrote to say that they are having a problem with sapsuckers attacking their trees. They make patches of little holes on the trunks and thus cause the tree to lose a lot of its sap, possibly killing the tree. She wondered if they could do anything about it outside of shooting the bird.

The only solution that I know of is to wrap the trunk of the tree with burlap in the spring when the sapsucker is most active and the sap in trees is rising. The burlap can be removed at a later date. If you have a lot of trees this might be a bit of a job, but as a rule the sapsucker has one or two favorite trees.

Orioles happily frequent hummingbird feeders and tank up on sweet water.

Snowy owls perch on tall objects to scout for food.

# Snowy Owls Winter in the South

My picture this week shows an arctic owl, sometimes called a snowy owl, perched on a roadside fence post. It has flown all the way from arctic regions where, during the summer, it dined on such rodents as lemmings, young rabbits and certain species of waterfowl and arctic birds.

Fall comes earlier to those regions above the tree line than it does here. Consequently birds start migrating south early. The lemmings and arctic hares remain, but if the population is low, then the snowy owl responds to its natural instincts and begins to move south. It travels over the great forests to the flat, open country such as our prairies and into the northern United States.

Each fall, on a chosen day in November, we will take a drive following the west shore of Last Mountain Lake. There are many rock piles in the adjoining fields, and that is where we will usually see a snowy perched on the highest rock in the pile. Once in a field we spotted a truck with a peculiar object on the end of its hood. We were a fair distance away, and so we thought it was something the owner had put there. Perhaps a gas can or some such thing. It looked dark from a distance, but as we got closer it turned out to be a snowy owl who chose to perch there.

One would think the arctic owl, because it is an owl, would want to be in a place where there were lots of trees. But the flat fields of the prairies resemble the arctic barrens, I suppose, and as this bird is truly a bird of the wide-open spaces it feels at home here.

Some of these owls will be almost immaculate white. These are mature males. Some will be heavily marked with dark brown, others more lightly so. Females are the darker marked and immature males the lighter.

Well, here we are into January. The shortest day of the year, December 22, is behind us and soon we will be noticing the sun staying with us a little longer each afternoon. The lengthening daylight will begin to trigger certain instincts in wild birds. Horned owls will begin to hoot more, signifying the approaching mating season. They do nest early, often in late February and early March.

There are records of grey jays (whisky jacks) nesting in January even if the temperature is -40°F, but March is more usual. Even then, the weather can be very cold.

At this time of year memories and pleasant times of summer are still with us.

Eileen Armstrong of Yorkton, Saskatchewan, wrote that she was with a group at Mustus Lake to fish. She was also watching birds and noticed eight large pelicans on the lake. They floated around, and sometimes one or two would fly off but soon would return. Armstrong was wondering if they were males or if there could be that many mated pairs on that little lake in early June.

I would say that these were non-breeding or bachelor birds. A pelican has to be two or three years of age before it starts to mate.

Michael Thomas of Yorkton wrote to tell of some of the wildlife that he has seen in his area. "My parents and I went fishing at the Lake-of-the-Prairies on the Assiniboine River in September. Our favorite spot is near the Saskatchewan-Manitoba border.

"Upon arrival we noticed some large white birds in the distance. A look through the binoculars confirmed that it was a flock of about 20 pelicans resting on a small sand bar. We also saw cormorants, Canada geese, ravens, a kingfisher, a bittern, a great blue heron and about half a dozen turkey vultures, positively identified by their red heads.

"The vultures were rotating round and around on lofty wind currents. We were very surprised to see them there.

"The Assiniboine River area is abundant with wildlife and also many wildflowers and beautiful trees. In the fall the hillsides are ablaze with color. Around our farm area we always have lots of barn swallows, robins, both sharp-tailed and ruffed grouse, not to mention a variety of woodpeckers, such as sapsuckers, flickers, downy and hairy woodpeckers. The list goes on, which includes foxes, coyotes, deer, garter snakes and porcupines."

Here is an interesting note from Victor Hockley of Brandon, Manitoba. "One Sunday my wife and I were coming home from church around noon hour. It was a cold January morning. A flock of partridge flew up in front of the car and I happened to hit one. As I looked into the rear view mirror I saw it fluttering on the road so I backed up intending to put it out of its suffering.

"I was just stooping down when swoosh, a hawk came down and practically took it out of my hand. For a split second we looked each other in the eye. I imagine he was really hungry to do a thing like that."

# Magnificent Monarchs

**Subtle differences separate the viceroy butterfly from this one, the monarch.**

My picture of the monarch butterfly was taken with a 100 mm lens plus a close-up attachment. I haven't had the pleasure of seeing a monarch butterfly too often, but now and then I do. A few columns ago I wrote how an oriole flying through the trees reminded me of a flying piece of flame. Well, I would say the vibrant color of the monarch is a good match for the oriole.

It is indeed a beautiful butterfly and deserves the name of monarch. There is another one that is almost a dead ringer for the monarch in color; it is called a viceroy. The difference is it is a bit smaller and has one row of white spots on the wing border instead of two. There is also a black line crossing each hind wing outward from the middle. This line is fainter in the more northern specimens, says Ron Hooper in his book *Butterflies in Saskatchewan*.

The close appearance to the monarch apparently is for protection because the monarch is unpalatable to any predator that may choose to dine upon it. But it is reported that mice and two species of birds do prey upon it.

The monarch is one butterfly that, like birds, migrates south for the winter. Thousands go to California, while others migrate to Mexico. According to an article that appeared in the Regina *Leader-Post* back in 1986, each year millions of these butterflies make a journey of more than 3000 miles from southeast Canada and eastern states to the forests of oyamel fir northwest of Mexico City.

The Mexican government has declared a reserve to keep farmers from destroying these trees on which the orange and black beauties find shelter in the winter. The farmers there previously harvested the trees as their main source of income. Scientists are not sure if the monarch could adapt to other conditions if the forest were destroyed.

The declaration of the reserve should be recognized as a big step forward that will allow future generations in the United States, Canada and Mexico to enjoy the beauty of the monarch and the spectacle of its migration.

The World Wildlife Fund has provided an average of more than $30,000 U.S. annually in the past several years for scientific research on the monarchs and to develop Monarca, a private Mexican organization, to protect them.

Butterflies born at the end of summer in North America arrive at the Mexican forests around November 1. It takes them about two months to reach their winter quarters from the northernmost sites.

Emil Stock told a good story about antelope in a recent letter. Once while working summerfallow, Stock saw an antelope playing with a large Russian thistle about three feet across. The antelope would charge the thistle and butt it away. Then he would back up and charge again.

Stock went on to tell of another time a herd of about 20 antelope walked across the field where he was working. In their wandering they flushed out a large jack rabbit. The rabbit wasn't very much afraid of them and sat down again. A couple of younger antelope went over to him and began to buck up and down behind him. The rabbit hopped two or three hops ahead and stopped again. After teasing him awhile the herd wandered away.

Stock went on to include a crow story. He says while working around the farm yard he noticed a crow sitting in a tree. It had eggs, but he didn't realize this so he loaded up his .22 rifle and took aim. It was a very long shot. The crow did not move. So he fired another two shots at it, and still it did not move. Stock cautiously approached the tree, but the crow did not fly away. It turned out that he had killed it with his first shot and the other two hit the mark as well.

He left it there and about three days later a very large flock of crows had gathered and much cawing was going on. Later when he got back home he told his wife about it and remarked that it must have been a crow funeral. His wife jokingly replied, “Well, yes, by the time all the relatives got there, it would take a few days.”

# Crows Have Earned a Bad Reputation

Crows, magpies and jays all belong to the same family. Magpies, blue jays and gray jays stay with us all winter, but crows migrate southward.

They are hardy in their own right. They migrate only to the middle United States, where they put up with a certain amount of winter. A few crows do stick around for the Canadian winter, usually in the vicinity of a city or town garbage dump.

In the fall crows gather into large flocks for their southward journey. In September or October it is not unusual to see flocks of 200 or 300 birds in a stubble field. In some migrational routes they gather into much larger flocks. Last October I saw a telecast from Hamilton, Ontario, that said more than 100,000 crows had invaded the area.

The sky was black with flying crows and trees were literally loaded with the birds. Their droppings were causing a problem, so officials fired noisemakers to get the crows to move on.

We generally regard crows as bad birds. They rob duck nests, as well as those of game and song birds. But they do good things to make up for the bad. They eat cutworms and wireworms as well as grasshoppers, crickets and noxious weed seeds. They also help clean up garbage around human habitation.

On the farm we looked forward to seeing or hearing the first crow back in the spring. Where I lived this always occurred around March 21, even if there was still a lot of snow around.

Ravens live in the northern wooded parts of the country. To the untrained eye they look almost exactly like crows; they are black, with slightly longer bodies than crows and with stouter beaks. In flight their tails are a different shape—wedged, with the middle feathers longer than the outer ones. Ravens often soar, which crows don't. Crows caw, while ravens make guttural croaks. In winter ravens often move out of their northern habitat and come southward, where observers could easily mistake them for crows.

Crows make good nests of twigs and sticks lined with soft grass and shredded bark. The eggs, four to seven, are greenish blue blotched with brown. Years ago I found a mallard duck nesting in an old crow's nest, while four feet above her was a crow nesting in a freshly built nest. How they made out in the end I am not sure, but I'll bet the duck nested successfully.

A crow makes an amusing pet. People used to claim if you split its tongue it would talk. This is cruel and does not work, but it will make the bird sound different. Crows are very intelligent. A number of years ago I was told of a crow that was raised as a pet. On a cold day when men were working outside, it picked up one of the men's gloves and flew up on the roof above them. Part of the glove protruded over the edge of the roof.

The owner got a long stick and reached up in an attempt to knock the glove down. The crow immediately pulled the glove back so he couldn't reach it.

Helen Ambler of Saskatoon wonders if it is a good idea to feed hummingbirds man-made syrup; is it as nutritious as their natural food? This is a difficult question to answer. While they partake of natural foods such as flower nectar, pollen and small insects, hummingbirds seem to thrive on man-made syrup and like to tank up on it before they take off on their long journey south.

Back in an earlier column, Rose Strand of Hudson Bay, Saskatchewan, remarked on some white roses she had seen growing in that district, and wondered if they might be a separate species. Joyce Lamont of Maidstone, Saskatchewan, asks if what Rose saw could be Rosa arkansana. "This is a dwarf rose that grows in Saskatchewan. It is white, or soft rose, or white with a mid-rib blush.

"It is only a few inches high but does hybridize with taller roses. Rosa arkansana is one of the parents of the Parkland roses being developed at Morden, Manitoba. Colonies of these used to grow thickly along road edges here but not every year. They, like the floral emblem of Saskatchewan (the western red lily), tend to come and go with the weather."

Crows gobble up lots of plant and animal pests, and clean up our garbage.

The Bohemian waxwing is larger and greyer than the cedar waxwing.

# The Bohemian Waxwing: Our Bird of Winter

A Metis lady recently remarked that a tree is a spiritual experience. I would say a look at many of nature's wonders is indeed a spiritual experience. This week's picture of a Bohemian waxwing feeding in a crabapple tree is also.

Bohemian waxwings love fruit. They love the fruit of the mountain ash so much they gorge themselves and sometimes get too groggy to fly in a straight line or at all. I am not sure if they are really intoxicated, but the juice or some substance in the mountain ash berry does have an effect on their nervous system. I'm sure if the berries contained alcohol, the human race would have found out a long time ago and there would be no fruit left on the tree for the birds.

As most of us know, the Bohemian waxwing is the bird of winter, whereas the cedar waxwing is the one we see in summer. But Mother Nature is tricky and she sometimes breaks the rules. A large flock of cedar waxwings was seen in Regina, Saskatchewan, in early December.

One year on the farm I had a flock of cedar waxwings wintering down at the creek. But usually it's the Bohemian waxwing that you are looking at in winter. It is larger and greyer than the cedar waxwing and the undertail coverts are chestnut in color, whereas the cedar waxwings' are yellow.

Barbara Thompson of Bulyea, Saskatchewan, had an interesting experience when she looked out of her window one December night. She saw a coyote walking around the base of the apple tree out in the yard. He would crouch down, then leap up into the branches of the tree to eat the fruit.

He then would jump down, walk around the tree two or three times and leap up into the tree again and repeat the performance. Barbara and her husband watched for 20 minutes before the coyote jumped back down and faded away into the darkness of the night.

Apparently it wasn't the first time the coyote visited the tree because Barbara said she had noticed tracks around the tree in the snow and there were no dogs in the vicinity.

Stan Sheard of Regina Beach, Saskatchewan, had an interesting experience in early December also, only his involved a couple of ruffed grouse. The female grouse was up in a mountain ash tree enjoying a lovely feed of berries while the cock grouse was on the ground under the tree. Instead of enjoying any fallen berries, he would strut around with his ruffs raised, wings drooping and tail fanned like a turkey gobbler.

The female finally flew to the ground, ignored the show-off and proceeded to walk down the road with the amorous male strutting close behind. A most comical sight. Sharp-tailed grouse will dance in the fall and ruffed grouse sometimes drum on a warm autumn day, but this little male was a real strutter.

Margaret Krutz of Endeavour, Saskatchewan, wrote about the interesting variety of winter birds she has around her place. She has a dozen blue jays who just love a good meal of popcorn, provided it has been popped in oil and not dry. She says the evening grosbeaks rule the roost while the beautiful pine grosbeaks hop around on the ground picking up the leftovers. As evening grosbeaks will eat bushels of sunflower seeds one would think pine grosbeaks would do the same, but it is not the case. They love the seeds of ash trees, which they split open with their stout beaks to get the tiny piece of meat inside. They relish mountain ash berries, crabapples and chokecherries. I have discovered they really go for flaxseed, whether it is presented in a feeding tray or spread on the ground.

Margaret said she has had dark-eyed juncos this winter. I am surprised, but I understand they remain all winter in Ontario and are called snowbirds in eastern parts.

# Chicken and Duck Traits Mix in the Coot

Coot eggs stay very clean because the incubating bird is constantly swimming.

My illustration today shows a black-looking duck. Some people call them mud hens, but they are more correctly called American coots. Male and female birds look identical, so which is male and which is female is rather hard to determine. One thing for sure is that the one who lays the eggs is the female. But it's somewhat difficult to catch a coot in the process of laying an egg.

Coots swim like ducks, but their feet are not webbed. Instead, they have lobes of skin down each side of their toes, which enables them to swim and run on the water quite well. When coots are spied close up through field glasses, one sees their white, chicken-like beaks, which are not a characteristic of ducks.

I also have found out that coots have a fondness for grain. I had sprinkled wheat to attract ducks to the front of the blind where I hid to take photographs. The coots seemed to enjoy the grain as much as the ducks did.

The coot's nest is built in shallow water and is made from an accumulation of dried vegetation, such as bulrushes and marsh grass. In any coot nest that I have seen the eggs have always been very clean, I suppose because the feet and breast of the incubating birds are clean and wet from swimming.

Helen Fast of Ruskin, British Columbia, and her husband have an acreage and home that is surrounded by deep forest out on the Dewdney Trunk Road. She sent in this account about a pygmy owl. It happened around November 1984.

"One day there was a thud against our patio door. I knew right away it must be a bird, but I was surprised to see this little owl. It had knocked itself out and when I picked it up its head hung limp and I said to my husband, 'It must have broken its neck.' My husband looked at it and said, 'It's dead.'

"I poured some water on its head, then tried to get some in its beak. I wrapped it in an old towel and put it in a small basket near the old woodstove, where it was nice and warm.

"An hour or so later I went to see what was happening. Well, there it was sitting on the edge of the basket blinking at me—what a surprise! My husband got an old bird cage and put it in there. I also added water and wild bird seed in case it was hungry.

"It was so cute and it had spots on the back of its head that looked like real eyes. At first we didn't know which was the front of its head. We made about five phone calls to wildlife offices ... and one of them told us it was a pygmy owl. And we were also told not to try feeding it seeds because all it wanted was mice. Well, where in the world would we be able to get wild mice—and live ones?

"We kept it overnight and it seemed all right and real lively. So next morning we let it go. It flew up and over the tall trees across the road and disappeared into the wild blue yonder. Then about five minutes later to our great amazement came a crash—the same thud against the patio doors! I said, 'Oh, no, it can't be, not again.' There lay the little owl, knocked out and head limp. My husband said, 'Well, this time it is dead.' I carried on the same procedure and again wrapped it up in a towel and into the basket beside the warm stove.

"A few hours later I went to check on it, and when I opened the towel it flew out with such a burst that it really startled me as it was so close to my face. It flew up into the loft and crashed against the glass door up there. Here I am dashing up the stairs crying, 'Oh, no! Oh, no! Not again.' Our cat was sleeping up there and I heard her jump after the crash. I assumed she had the owl, but when I got up there she had been startled by the noise and ran and hid under the eaves. Once again I picked up the little owl with his head hanging limp. Well, this time for sure I thought its neck must have been broken—all these crash knock-outs.

"So again it went back into the towel, the basket and beside the stove. Sure enough, after a little while there was fluttering in the basket and the little owl was lively again. This time I put it back into the cage and my husband put a piece of raw liver in there, hoping the owl would eat it, but it wouldn't touch it. We covered the cage up for the night. We kept it until about 5 p.m. the next day. It seemed bright and healthy and strong, so once again we let it loose. This time the owl flew across the yard and landed on a branch of a huge maple tree, where it sat for quite some time. After a while we looked to see if it was there and what a relief it was to see that it was gone. We went back into the house and said, 'Thank goodness that's over with.'

"There is a story or myth that comes from my ancestors from Europe that an owl is a bad omen, a bearer of sadness. If it perches on the rooftop of the dweller's home, it means a death in the family. If it sits on the barn it means an illness shall befall on this family. I am not superstitious but doesn't it seem strange for this little owl to come back twice to our house and hit the same door, especially when we have neighbors all around us?"

# A Flicker Comes Close to Chilly Death

My picture today shows a little horned grebe riding the waves of its watery home. This species of grebe commonly breeds and nests in many sloughs and marshy areas across the prairies. I used a 300 mm lens to take the picture.

Joy Regier of Coaldale, Alberta, wrote to say how much she enjoys the column and saves them all by tucking them into a loose-leaf scrapbook. She writes: "I live approximately 10 miles out of Lethbridge on the flat prairie. We farm 80 acres here raising alfalfa and wheat or barley. We also have a pasture next to the yard. The only trees around are shelterbelts around farms.

"One afternoon in the middle of April I was relaxing out on the lawn when I heard some kind of an unusual bird calling in the pasture and went to see. I couldn't believe it. There were turkeys, nine in all. These were wild turkeys. The gobbler was displaying himself. What a sight. I fetched my binoculars and watched them for a while. They were walking across the alfalfa and then the stubble, picking up seeds.

"Later on I drove out there but they were gone. The next day I heard that someone else had sighted them about two miles west of our farm.

"One of my brothers ranches about 30 miles west of Claresholm in the foothills, and in June of 1983 we sighted a wild turkey while driving across ranchland. My brother has seen them since, so they are surviving there."

I wasn't aware that wild turkeys were in southwestern Alberta. I presume they are on a wildlife management program.

Here is an interesting story from Joan Wooton of Langley, British Columbia. She writes: "Reading your story of the hungry owl back in the winter reminded me of an occasion in the late 1950s when in the early fall the ground was frozen solid with no snow cover.

"A mean, cold wind was blowing, and on looking out of the window I saw what at first looked like a ball of dead leaves rolling past on the ground. Suddenly I realized it must be a bird of some kind—about the size of a small owl.

"I rushed out and followed it to the neighbor's back door, where it just sat helplessly, quite unable to move. On picking it up I recognized it as a red-shafted flicker, but it was so starved it could not have weighed more than an ounce.

"I put it in a laundry tub, covering it with a screen, and after an hour or so it seemed to be warm enough to perk up. I fed it cat food, which it readily swallowed, and by the next morning it seemed well on the way to recovery, as it was soon able to peck the cat food on its own and drink water.

"I let it loose in the room in a few days, and found it was able to fly to the window. After a couple of weeks it had gained so much in weight and strength I let it go free outside, but it remained around for several months, coming to our bird feeder regularly. It was a thrilling experience to have rescued this beautiful wild creature from what surely was almost certain death."

It can be noted that Joan remarked that it was a red-shafted flicker. Here on the prairies we have the yellow-shafted flicker. In Alberta and even the western parts of Saskatchewan there is a blending of the two species. So it is possible to see both the yellow- and red-shafted.

Alex Miklos of Edmonton, Alberta, wrote an interesting letter regarding a yellow-bellied sapsucker. He writes: "Two years ago on the home farm we had a pail on a short post close to the house. Every day a woodpecker would come and drum on the pail. This would happen early in the morning and at different times during the day.

"He kept this up from early spring till the beginning of August. It appeared he could not attract a mate, as he always seemed to be alone. Not far away from where he drummed on the pail were small Saskatoon trees. When he got tired of drumming he flew to the Saskatoon trees where he made holes in straight lines on the trunks of the trees and sucked or drank the sap.

"There were a lot of trees and every one was damaged with holes straight up and down and crosswise. On a maple tree not too far away he also made a pattern of holes on the trunk. But the Saskatoon trees must have had a sweeter sap, for it was there that I saw bees and ants apparently feeding on the sap, but not on the maple.

"I don't know if that bird is classified as a woodpecker or something else, as he appeared to live on tree sap all the time he was there."

What you have there is a yellow-bellied sapsucker. It is a species of woodpecker but he was apparently made to be a lover of sap. It does, however, nest in holes in trees, as other woodpeckers do. It can become a real nuisance if you have fruit trees in your yard or a cut-leaf birch.

The horned grebe builds its nest in sloughs and marsh areas.

# Unhurried Hawks Fly South

At this time of year Swainson's hawks are many miles south of their nesting grounds in the prairie provinces. They spend the winter as far south as Argentina, and some may be there now. That is a long way to fly, but the flight is gradual. They don't try to do it in a matter of a few days, unlike fast-flying ducks or geese, who are capable of making their flight south in jig time.

In late August and early September I enjoy driving down a back road and seeing two or three of these big, beneficial hawks perched on telephone poles or fence posts. They are quite trusting and will allow a fairly close approach if you are in a vehicle. This is especially true if they are immature.

This is how I got today's picture. There were at first three birds, but just as I was focusing the lens one flew away. I used my 70–210 zoom lens and, as usual, the film was Kodachrome 64.

Swainson's and red-tailed hawks are true friends of humans, for they destroy huge numbers of rodents during the summer, especially during the time they are feeding young. These little ones grow fast and require a tremendous amount of food.

It is said that these hawks get their vitamins from the fur and feathers of their prey. These are not digested but are regurgitated in the form of pellets, along with bones and other hard-to-digest parts. By examining these pellets we can determine what kind of animal the hawk had for breakfast.

Mrs. M. Friederici of Arborg, Manitoba, wrote about an interesting experience. "The grandchildren, my daughter and myself had our picnic table close in the shade of a dense birch tree in the park area on the north point of Hecla Island. We had been roasting wieners and three wiener buns remained in a plastic bag. The children took to the swings while the two of us leaned back in our chairs to absorb some sun and rest.

"Suddenly out of the birch tree a crow landed on the table. He just picked up the plastic bag with the wiener buns and flew off into the nearby woods. What a big surprise!

"We had observed our surroundings and there was no sign of anything, not even a bird. The crow must have been in the tree watching every move and biding his time. We are still wondering if the crow managed to get the buns through the plastic bag."

Our prairie crows are pretty smart fellows and know when good pickings are afoot. With that strong beak I am quite sure Mr. Crow would have little difficulty getting through the bag to the buns.

On the subject of hawks, here is an observation sent in by Eileen Bennetto of Piapot, Saskatchewan. She writes: "I want to tell you about an interesting experience my daughter and I had with a young hawk last fall. We noticed it sitting by the tractor wheel that was parked down below the house. It stood there for the longest time so we went down to investigate. I threw my gloves at it but it wouldn't move. Then we noticed a snake wrapped around its legs.

"Just then two pheasant hunters came into the yard and one of them came over to see what was going on. He grabbed the hawk by the wing tips, and at the same time I stepped on the snake's tail. Finally after a steady tug the snake and the hawk became 'unhooked' and the hawk flew off a short distance. He stood for a while, then walked a short distance before flying off. He seemed bewildered by it all, but he never made any effort to strike at us or get loose from the thing on his own at any time."

This hawk must have tried to pick up the snake but things backfired and the snake entwined around the hawk's legs. If he had captured the snake in his talons in the first place he probably would have been able to make off with it.

Eve Torbitt of Chapman, Saskatchewan, writes: "On August 20, while my husband was swathing a wheat field, he came across a fawn hiding in the wheat. He wasn't sure whether it was a fawn or a baby antelope, since we do have a small herd of antelope making their home in our fields. It was dark brown with a spotted back.

"It didn't want to leave the shelter of the wheat, and after he chased it back and forth for a minute it did sprawl flat on its belly and seemed to think it was invisible in that position. Finally he managed to shoo it out of there and into an adjacent field of wheat.

"He started the swather again and almost immediately came upon another one smaller than the first. After he chased this one back and forth it did the same sprawl and refused to get up. He spoke quietly to it, then gently gathered it up in his arms. It was about the size of a tom cat. It lay limp in his arms until he set it down in the wheat with the other one, then with a loud Ba-Ba-Ba, it scampered away."

These were deer fawns, as the young of antelope do not have any spots.

Young Swainson's hawks require a tremendous amount of food.

# Pintail Ducks Arrive Early

If the pintail drake were to suspect danger, he'd stretch his neck to look around.

A very handsome duck illustrates this column. It is a male pintail drake. The name is derived from the two middle tail feathers that extend out longer than the others and come to a long, slender point. Only the tail of the drake is designed this way; the tail of the female is only slightly pointed.

If you have seen any ducks flying across the prairie skies this March, they are more than likely pintails, as they arrive early. Mallards, redheads and shovelers follow later.

The male pintail is so gracefully made and so beautifully marked.

The long, slender beak allows the bird to reach down a little deeper into the water to feed, and the tail does not tip up as often as in other species. If there is a suspicion of an intruder approaching, the male's neck suddenly stretches upward, allowing the bird to scan the surroundings to its best advantage. The whole body becomes tense and ready to explode into the air.

I took this photo from the concealment of a blind by the shore of a slough, using a 300 mm lens. The drake and his friends had no idea at all that a human was anywhere near, and what a pleasure it was to watch them under this condition.

These trim greyhounds of the duck family nest all across the prairies. On the farm I would often flush a nesting pintail from a patch of tall stubble or a growth of buck brush. They are tight nesters, and often the hen wouldn't flush till she was almost stepped on, and then she would come out with a roar of wings, startling me half to death. The nest hollow would hold up to 10 eggs, quite buff in color.

The other day while walking along the lakeshore I saw fresh skunk tracks in the snow. By the look of the track he was making good time loping right along. The tracks reminded me of someone talking about coming across a skunk that had its head stuck in a glass jar. A day later a letter came from Oscar Torwalt of Love, Saskatchewan, who tells of a similar case with a woodchuck.

As a foreman for a Saskatchewan Natural Resources fire crew, he and his crew were doing some cleaning up at a few of the campgrounds northeast of White Fox. "At lunch time on this particular day, we were sitting in one of the camp kitchens when we heard a noise that sounded like a tin can hitting a tree. In that quiet atmosphere, it sounded unnatural and weird. The sound came closer and closer with every bang. Suddenly one fellow said, 'Look, there's a tin can and it's moving!'

"We went to investigate, and here was an animal with a tomato can over its head. Naturally it couldn't see where it was going and kept bumping into a tree. I got my gloves and we pulled the can off its head—it was a groundhog or woodchuck.

"At first it ran away about 12 feet, then stopped and turned around and looked at us straight in the eye as if to say thank you. It slowly turned around and left. We never saw the animal again."

# Marsh Hawks Become Good Hunters

In an earlier column, my photograph featured a female marsh hawk in flight. Today we have young marsh hawks that have just hatched. They are so cute, almost like baby chickens all covered with fawnish down.

However, the cute phase does not last long, and two weeks later they are ugly, but become beautiful birds of prey once they feather out. Their back and wing feathers are chocolate brown while the breast and underparts are a burnt orange. They soon learn to fly on long, slender wings as their parents do, searching for mice, voles, frogs and grasshoppers.

There is one little mammal that few people see or even think about: the shrew. It is so small that it could crawl through a finger ring.

Hazel Paton of Oxbow, Saskatchewan, mentioned that she had one under her house but hasn't seen it since a weasel took up residence there. No need to worry about mice or rats under your house if you have a weasel.

Clifford Hill of Fernie, British Columbia, says he has seen quite a few shrews this past winter. This gives a pretty good indication of how widespread the range of the shrew is.

The shrew is a very small mouse-like creature. It is not related to the mouse family, but is a species by itself. It has a long narrow snout and a short tail.

There are at least 53 sub-species of shrews listed in H.E. Anthony's *Field Book of North American Mammals*. The water shrew is quite a bit larger than the other variety. The shrew we have in the Canadian provinces is listed as the pigmy shrew—the smallest one of all.

Shrews are very secretive and most active at night but do come out occasionally to hunt in the daytime. Lift up a log and you just might find one of these little creatures. They are by no means retiring when confronted by an animal larger than themselves, such as a mouse or vole. It will attack, kill and eat them. But, of course, they're no match for a weasel.

Anthony says mice put into a cage with a shrew are dispatched with a certainty that indicates this is by no means a new experience for the shrew. Put two shrews in a cage together and one will kill the other. They are small but ferocious little beasts. They are active all winter long but they do have to eat often because of a very rapid rate of digestion. Deprived of food for even a few hours, they will starve to death. That's something like hummingbirds, who have to feed almost steadily during their waking hours.

Edna Stoltz of Tomahawk, Alberta, says she saw a blue jay robbing the dog dish of food pellets. She noticed that he was pecking at the ground and she thought he had accidently dropped a morsel but was amazed to see the jay pick up the pellet and drop it in the hole that he had pecked in the ground. Then the bird reached out and lifted two or three dried leaves and carefully placed them over the hole. She watched him do this around the yard. She wonders if this is a usual procedure of a jay.

I have never actually seen a jay do this, but I do know that they will take food such as peanuts or sunflower seeds, pack it into their mouths and fly away to hide it. I wonder if they are storing it for a rainy day and also if they really remember where they put it. They are very smart, so I wouldn't be surprised if they do remember.

At this time of year, butterflies will be emerging from their cocoons. Beth L. Tachit of Hines Creek, Alberta, wrote about a friend who made a special point of growing milkweed for the larvae of the monarch butterfly to feed on. Many cocoons hung on the weeds in her garden and were checked every morning.

If any had fallen to the ground, her friend came with a silk thread and tied them up again. The butterflies wouldn't emerge properly on the ground and would be unable to spread their wings and fly. She said watching them emerge each morning was a very memorable experience.

In my opinion the monarch is the most beautiful butterfly of all.

Baby marsh hawks don't remain cute for long.

The snowshoe hare or bush rabbit changes
from brown in summer to white in winter.

# This Hare Wears Shoes and Changes Coats

I looked out the window one morning and saw a little brown bush rabbit eating some lawn clover. I enjoyed watching him having his breakfast of fresh green leaves. There was no doubt about it, rabbits are cute and have their own special appeal.

This rabbit enjoyed the clover so much he came for several mornings about the same time. Of course I just had to take advantage of the situation and shoot a few pictures. So taking the camera, equipped with 150 mm lens and Kodachrome 64 film, I stole out a door on the far side, then carefully tiptoed around the east wall to the south side where the bunny was located. I peeked around the corner cautiously, and there he was, stomach filled and quite content.

The proper name for a bush rabbit is a varying hare because it is a hare and its coat varies from brown in summer to white in winter. Because of its large hind feet it is also called the snowshoe rabbit. The hairy feet spread out considerably when traveling over snow and act as snowshoes.

We call it a bush rabbit because it lives in the bush, not out on open plains as do the jackrabbits. Varying hares usually have three to four young in a litter but they may have as many as eight or 10, which causes the increase they are noted for. There is evidence to show they could have more than one litter per year.

The white snowshoe rabbit in the other photo, taken 10 months later, is just starting its spring moult, shedding its white winter fur to reveal the brown summer fur.

In my opinion, these little rabbits are anything but born lucky—they are food for so many other wild creatures, such as owls, foxes, coyotes, hawks, weasels and humans. Rabbit stew and fried rabbit are both tasty.

I was following the fresh tracks of a snowshoe rabbit one day on new-fallen snow. As the tracks crossed over an open space they just suddenly quit, as if the animal had just taken wing. Then I realized that it had suddenly become airborne, but not on its own power—it had been taken by a great horned owl. About two feet on each side of the tracks there were marks where the owl's wings had lightly touched the snow as it scooped up the rabbit.

Another time I saw where a weasel had surprised and caught a snowshoe. The death struggle was marked in the snow, and the body of the rabbit still lay there. The weasel had eaten into the throat and chest cavity. My sympathy goes out to the victim of a predator, although some predators are victims of larger predators. Nature is very cruel, or so it appears to us humans. Perhaps we simply don't understand nature's way.

# Wrens Stuff Twigs into Handy Spots

A wren's small eggs are guarded in cramped quarters.

Today's picture shows the nest and eggs of the common house wren. The eggs are small but beautifully marked with brownish red spots or dots.

Wrens will nest in the oddest places at times. They will also make false nests—nests they never really intend to use. Sometimes on the farm when my overalls hung on the clothesline for a day or two, a wren would stuff a pocket full of twigs. I often wondered if they were left for any length of time if a real nest with eggs would be built.

I recall an old coffee pot hung on a snag of a tree down by the creek.

Each year a wren would build her nest and rear her young in it.

House wrens will nest at times in very small and cramped quarters. I am thinking of a round cedar fence post on the farm. It had a diameter of no more than four inches. It had stood in the ground for years, so long that the core of the post eventually rotted away and the side of the post split open, leaving a crack of about three-quarters of an inch wide. A house wren had squeezed in there and built her nest.

Needless to say it contained very few twigs. Often when passing by I would peer into the crack, and if the light was right I'd see the bird's tiny bright eye peering out at me.

Wrens are such perky and lively little creatures and are great singers, but they do have one bad habit on occasion that mars their character, and that is they become jealous of other birds nesting nearby and will puncture their eggs with their slender little beaks. As I said, they don't always do this, but once in a while they will.

There are other kinds of wrens besides the house wren. There are two varieties of marsh wrens: the short-billed and the long-billed. There is also the rock wren and the winter wren. But the house wren is the one that is favored and loved by us all.

Connie Bevans of Carrot River, Saskatchewan, has written to tell about an owl that was found dead, killed by a car or electrocuted by a power line. As it was just freshly killed she took it home and had it stuffed, and it is now a prize possession. She didn't actually say what kind of an owl it was, but if it was quite large and had tufts of feathers protruding from the top of its head it would be a great horned owl. She wonders where such a bird would nest.

Great horned owls and long-eared owls never make a nest of their own but will use the nest of some other large bird. A great horned owl will nest in a hawk's nest, and the long-eared owl will use a crow's nest.

# The Loon Sounds So Mournful and Wild

I suppose most readers have heard the wild primeval cry of the common loon. Here, at Last Mountain Lake, a few loons each spring will land to rest and even remain a week or two, but we seldom hear them call. In fact, if I remember correctly, I only heard them once last spring. But if you go to a forest-rimmed lake farther north you will hear them for sure. It appears this species simply has to have a body of water that is forest-bound and away from the hustle and bustle of the open southern communities.

I photographed this pair of common loons with my 300 mm lens in Prince Albert National Park in the month of May. That particular day, when we left here at Regina Beach to go to the park, Last Mountain Lake was completely ice-free; boats were already bouncing around on its surface and the aspen poplars in the ravines of the hills were all dressed out in fresh green leaves.

But arriving in the park we found spring had arrived much later, for there were no green leaves nor any catkins starting to develop on the aspens. The lakes were still frozen except for around the edge, where it was starting to thaw and there would be a band of water measuring from 10 to 30 feet wide. It was in this edge of water that we were surprised to find loons swimming. I guess they just could not wait to get to their summer home.

In one of the wider areas of water we counted six loons, and it was while we were watching them that we heard loons from farther down the shore give out their wild, lonely cries. Then to our delight the ones we were watching called in answer.

To hear loons cry at such close range is an experience, but in my opinion their sounds are most haunting in the evening when the water is calm and the forest is still, with perhaps only the nervous chirping of a bird or squirrel to break the silence. Then from somewhere far away the cry of the loon floats across the water—so mournful yet so wild. It is almost as if some ancient spirit had suddenly awakened from the distant past and was calling out its complaints.

There are other loons besides the common loon that one just might be lucky enough to see during the season of migration; there is the red-throated loon and the Arctic loon. We won't see them in summer unless we take a trip and really go north, for it is in those far northern reaches, even all the way to the Arctic, that these species breed and nest. Both these loons are smaller than the common loon. Of the three species I would say the latter one is the most attractive with its large size and jet-black and sparkling white markings.

We have all heard of the expression "crazy as a loon." The loon itself is just as sane as any other bird, its wild call (some people call it a laugh) gave rise to the expression.

If a loon is forced down in a storm while migrating, it pretty well is curtains for the poor bird, for once it is on the ground there is no way it can get airborne again. To take to the air it has to be on water, where it makes a long run to get flying. The loon is not like a duck, which can go straight into a flight from a standing start.

People paddling canoes may find the nest of the common loon located in marshy areas of the lake. Usually the nest is a heap of vegetation, although the birds might use an old muskrat house squashed down flat or, more rarely, may nest on the ground at the edge of the water. A clutch will comprise only two large, olive-brown eggs, which are sparsely spotted with black.

With good old April here now, we know that another long winter has passed and we have an exciting spring and summer to look forward to. The crows are cawing again, bluebirds are on the wing and wildflowers will soon be blooming. Spring is such a wonderful time of year!

I wonder if there is such a thing as a butterfly farmer in Saskatchewan. Not likely! It seems to me I had a letter or two a few years ago from someone who was interested in such a thing in either Manitoba or Ontario. Apparently down in the States there are a few. Calvin Myers of New Jersey is one. It all began 18 years ago when as a boy he captured an emerald caterpillar, put the insect in a jar and watched as it became a chrysalis and then a colorful butterfly.

From that time on Myers was hooked, and he and his family began raising butterflies. He raises them on nine hectares in Denville. The farm's most unique feature is the white gauze nets that are strung over tree limbs to provide protection for the caterpillars from their many enemies.

Caterpillars, some of which grow to seven inches in length, have voracious appetites and eat day and night. Tree leaves, especially wild cherry, maple, birch and sassafras, attract the insects to the garden. Some of them feed on weeds such as clover and dandelion. Mating butterflies can be a tricky business. Some only mate in the rain and some only mate when there is a storm coming. One of the satisfactions that Myers gets from raising butterflies is the enjoyment they bring to other people, especially school students.

The loon must be in the water before it can take to the air.

# Indian Paintbrush Bracts Provide Brilliant Color

The Indian paintbrush grows in moist woodland meadows and some parkland.

Indian paintbrush—what a beautiful and interesting plant. Not a plant of the wild open spaces, but of moist woodland meadows and certain areas of the parklands. There are seven or eight species of paintbrush, but the kind in my picture seems to be the most common in north woodlands.

In the foothills of the Rocky Mountains, and in the mountains themselves, I've seen paintbrush plants that were a brilliant red. Although they are listed for our northern treed area, I haven't yet been fortunate enough to see them there.

It's not the flower itself that gives the plant its color, it's the colorful bracts that are below each flower and hide them from view. Even the calyx is commonly more colored. Watch for them in our national and provincial parks.

People flock to these parks by the thousands because of the trees and lakes. Trees are indeed a spiritual experience. They do so much to make our countryside beautiful. The smell of the woods can't be beat and the evergreens have a most appealing aroma.

We can't always go to the northern woodlands, but we can make miniature ones at our farms and homes simply by planting trees. The more trees, the more birds and other forms of nature.

A pamphlet entitled "How the Forest Grows" reveals some interesting facts about trees. On a warm summer day, for instance, the leaves of a large tree can suck up from its roots as much as two or three hundred gallons of water. Trees for all their great bulk and strength can be up to 90 percent water.

The needles of a conifer tree are its leaves, and they function the same as the broad-leafed deciduous trees. The outer layer of a needle is a waxy film that helps protect the trees in dry weather.

The surface of the needle is covered with pores, called stomata, which help in the transpiration of excess moisture. But, if the tree is not actively feeding by photosynthesis, the pores will close to conserve moisture. Just under the surface of a needle is the layer of green chlorophyll that captures the energy of the sun and uses it to create food.

The bark of a tree is its coat of armor. When attacked by pests or injured by fire or storm, evergreens heal the wound in the bark with a secretion of pitch.

Yellow-bellied sapsuckers had drilled a pattern of holes in the trunk of my tree, and although it was a fair piece of patchwork, the holes soon filled and were sealed with pitch.

Every tree has two layers of bark, an inner layer and an outer layer. The inner bark is soft and moist, which allows food to pass up and down the trunk and into the branches. It is this inner bark that rodents such as porcupines like to feed on in the winter because of the rich food value.

The older the tree gets, the thicker the bark becomes. In fact, in the case of Douglas firs in British Columbia, the bark may become as thick as one foot.

According to an article by Bruce Obee in *Beautiful British Columbia* magazine, there is a Douglas fir on the west coast of Vancouver Island with the amazing height of over 95 feet. Its age is estimated at 400 years. Think of the weight of this tree held by a terrific root system. And what a view an eagle or whatever would get when perched on the top tip.

Tree roots have three jobs to do. They are the principal source of water, they absorb essential minerals and they are the tree's anchor, holding it erect despite storms and gales. Some trees develop a tap root at the start of growth that disappears as the tree matures. Fir trees are an example of this.

Tree nurseries inform us that when planting young trees, we must be sure the roots are well spread out. If not, as the tree grows it will not be well anchored.

# Butterflies Never Stay Still

**A bright alfalfa butterfly perches on a shasta daisy.**

My picture today shows an alfalfa butterfly perched on a flower. This butterfly is so named because of its fondness for alfalfa plants. This particular specimen likes other plants as well. The flower it is perched on is a shasta daisy. As I have so often said, butterflies are not easy subjects to photograph, mainly because they are not easy to approach.

Then, too, when one has made a close approach and is ready to press the shutter, a breeze will spring up and the subject will sway out of focus, and more than likely the butterfly will fly away.

But it is good sport and a real challenge to one's patience. To get the picture I used my 100 mm lens with a bellows attachment. Kodachrome 64 was the film used.

The alfalfa butterfly belongs to a group known as the sulphurs. According to Hooper in his book *Butterflies of Saskatchewan*, the specimens of July and August are large and brightly colored, whereas those of October are smaller and somewhat duller.

The larvae or caterpillars are grass green with an indistinct stripe down the back, a white stripe edged below with black along the side. Too many caterpillars could do some damage, but this usually is not the case.

It's not very often we get letters from Ontario, so it was nice to receive one recently from Mrs. Ivan Bjorklund, who lives at Ignac, Ontario. She wrote as follows: "The excerpt from a letter in your Prairie Wildlife column, in which Wilma Pierce tells of an eagle taking a bath, prompts me to tell you of my experience of seeing the tiniest bird, a hummingbird, take a bath.

"The hummingbird is not so plentiful here in northwestern Ontario as on the prairies. But with a feeder out for them all summer we are able to attract a few to our yard every year. They enjoy the tall evergreens surrounding our yard also. One real hot afternoon when I was using the watering hose to water my garden I noticed a hummingbird dart in and out of the spray apparently quite agitated. After he repeated his performance several times, I turned the nozzle to a fine spray, keeping my movements slow and very still. Much to my delight, the hummingbird took a bath in the misty spray, hovering in one place in mid-air. His washing procedure was much the same as a bird bathing in a puddle. When finished, he flew to a dead twig of a raspberry cane to dry off, preening and drying his feathers. I wonder if hummingbirds bathe in rain showers instead of on the ground?

"One of our favorite fishing spots is under a large concrete bridge spanning a river where the swallows nest underneath. This particular day in early May, all was silent as the birds had not yet arrived from the south. Suddenly the air was filled with exciting critters as with one swoop a flock of 100 or more swallows was back. They darted in and out of all the previous summer nests, seemingly overjoyed at reaching the end of their flight.

"This is another experience I should never forget as afterwards the birds settled down a bit and were not filled with such exuberant rejoicing, even though it seemed they were never still as they flew in and out under the bridge singing and twittering all the time.

"Coming from central Manitoba we notice that the birds are not as numerous here even in the summer. But with a feeder out all winter we do attract chickadees, both boreal and black-capped, whisky jacks (grey jays), hairy and down woodpeckers, blue jays, pine grosbeaks and nuthatches. Evening grosbeaks will always be present if they have had the inclination to stay in the area for the winter."

Now we will travel many miles from northwest Ontario all the way up to Whitehorse, Yukon. From here a letter came from Tracy Harris, who writes as follows:

"My father, Nick Kotyk of Red Deer, Alberta, forwards *Western People* to me knowing how much I enjoy the supplement to *The Western Producer*. Prairie Wildlife is usually a first when I open the pages.

"I live on Lake LeBarge (the same lake Robert Service wrote about in his poem 'The Cremation of Sam McGee').

"The redpolls arrived at my cabin on March the 10th this year, one full month earlier than other years. I usually put out finch food for them, as they seem to prefer smaller seeds. This year I noticed they were also utilizing the feeder, which the black-capped and boreal chickadees, as well as the downy and hairy woodpeckers, frequent.

"This feeding station has bags of beef suet and peanut butter, and I was so surprised to see the redpolls there among the chickadees, woodpeckers and juncos.

"The mountain bluebird arrived April 5, much to my dismay, as the ground was blanketed in three feet of snow. And just the week before my dog had ripped a down-filled sleeping bag off the clothesline with feathers all over that will make great nesting materials for the birds this spring.

"I have also put up 28 bluebird nesting boxes on the Klondike Highway. Nine of these were occupied last year by bluebirds and some by tree swallows."

# Geese Spring to the Nest

A mother goose sits comfortably on her nest of six white eggs in today's photo. The nest is heavily lined with down that she plucked from her own breast. It not only makes a snug nest but is used to cover and conceal the eggs from predators when she's away.

By now, there may be little goslings hatched and swimming behind mother and dad goose. Geese, like ducks, don't waste any time starting to nest when they return in the spring. The eggs hatch after 30 days of incubation.

It's great to see spring again, the fields starting to turn green, the blue of the crocus in the pasture and the meadowlarks singing from their favorite fenceposts.

The ice has gone out of the lake and people are out in their boats. Farther north it will be a little different; lakes may be still covered by rotting ice. But the juncos, tree sparrows, thrushes and white-throated sparrows will brighten the woodlands with their cheery songs.

In southern parts, tree swallows and bluebirds are peeking into bird boxes and choosing their nesting locations.

Here are a few recent letters that need to be shared. Hazel Reves of Holbein, Saskatchewan, writes: "For the third winter we have had a one-legged hairy woodpecker feeding at our suet. His movements are quite lurchy and he is a bit larger than the others.

"The leg appears to have been placed quite centrally so I deduce Mother Nature goofed but good. Preening must be next to impossible, as the feathers look rough and scruffy. To try and preen, he would indeed roll like a tumbleweed in the breeze. A gusty wind does blow him from his buffet, but he flips up to dine again."

Mother goose used her own down to luxuriously line her nest.

# These Predators Enjoy Fresh Meat

The bill of the male evening grosbeak turns green as spring approaches.

I took this week's photo of an evening grosbeak a year or two ago with my 300 mm lens. Some readers have reported to me they have evening grosbeaks dining on sunflower seeds at their feeders this winter. So far none has appeared at mine.

The reason for this may be the lack of natural food in our area. We had a late heavy frost that took a big toll on wild berries and the seeds of trees.

Evening grosbeaks are northern forest birds in the summer. We in southern parts see them only in the winter. Around a feeding station they are indeed a noisy and excited group. I have noticed that as spring approaches the bills of the males take on a decided greenish tinge.

The post has brought in some interesting letters.

Elizabeth Josuttes of Paradise Hill, Saskatchewan, wrote to tell about a weasel getting into the barn and killing a hen. A week or two later it came back and killed a rooster. This time, however, the weasel fell victim to the cat.

Elizabeth asks the question: "What do weasels do after they are filled up from their kill?" In answer to this I would say weasels are very active both winter and summer. They use up a lot of energy, especially during the colder months, and must feed often.

A weasel has a route or range in which it travels. After killing a hen, and feeling well fed, it probably curls up and sleeps somewhere for a few hours, then travels on again. In a week or so it will travel back over its route and, remembering its previous good feed from the hen, will try for another capture at the same location.

Elizabeth goes on to tell about a great horned owl that preyed on her tame rabbits. She said she found that the head of one rabbit was missing, but the rest of the body was intact. After two rabbits were killed she kept the rest of the rabbits penned up. She wonders if the beheading is always part of the way the big owl makes its kill.

As far as I can determine, when a bird of prey makes a kill it will usually start dining on the soft throats of the victim, especially if it's the size of a rabbit. The head is then quickly removed. Because the head of the rabbit is the lightest of the two remaining parts, I would say the owl chose to fly away and feed upon it. The skull and jaw bones of the rabbit are quite large and one would think difficult to swallow. Yet the owl is a powerful bird and has the capability of swallowing large objects. Bones of mammals are found in the pellets that the horned owl regurgitates.

Owls, like most birds of prey, prefer their meat freshly killed, and it is very unlikely they would come back to a frozen carcass. I know of a Cooper's hawk that killed a pigeon. However, before it could dine it was disturbed and flew away. This was in early spring and the weather was very cold. The next day I was surprised to see the hawk back at the frozen body of the pigeon. There are exceptions to all the rules.

Kathleen Johnstone lives in the open plains country of Francis, Saskatchewan. Other than farm shelterbelts, there are very few if any trees, so she doesn't have the chance of seeing many winter woodland birds. However, before Christmas a black-capped chickadee appeared in her yard. This, she says, is the first time she has seen this species there and regarded it as a real treat.

Chickadees are favorites with many people. In wooded and parkland-type country they are with us all winter long, and no matter how bad the weather they are always friendly, happy and cheerful.

Doreen Grahn of Marwayne, Alberta, wrote to tell of different natural occurrences around her place in the past year or so.

"The swallows were back last spring and were very busy packing mud under the eaves of the house. When the nest was finished they were sent off by a pair of phoebes who had nested in an outbuilding for two or three years. Last summer they got lazy, but I cheered for them when the poor swallows had to start over again in an old granary.

"They raised a family of four and the young were so cute when they peeked over the edge of their mud nests.

"Then the strawberry patch was being robbed, and at first I blamed the robins, but watching closely in the morning to determine what small thief went under the leaves for the fruit, the soft "zee-zee" notes soon gave the masked bandits away. They were cedar waxwings. They dearly love berries, especially fresh, ripe ones.

"While out checking a wheat crop last summer the screaming of a hawk drew my attention, and so I answered. Each time she screamed I answered again, and soon she circled nearer and nearer. This was the closest I had one come to me.

"So far this winter I have had six blue jays coming to the feeder. Also good numbers of evening and pine grosbeaks."

# Pronghorns Were Once Near Extinction

Pronghorn antelope used to number between 40 million and 60 million in North America.

One of the prettiest of wild animals, as far as I'm concerned, is the pronghorn antelope. Often it is simply referred to as pronghorn. Ranchers and farmers of southwest Saskatchewan and southern parts of Alberta are used to seeing pronghorns and consider them no novelty. To other people, they are indeed a novelty and most interesting. I am told that years ago, before the prairies fell under the plow, the range of the pronghorn was much greater and they were common in the Qu'Appelle Valley and Last Mountain Lake areas of Saskatchewan and perhaps even beyond. It has been estimated that at one time the total population of these antelope in North America was somewhere between 40 million and 60 million.

Today's herds are but a small remnant due to the white man's settlement and relentless slaughter. One report claims that in Saskatchewan the pronghorn became virtually extinct in the early 1900s, but through careful management they have returned to a population of about 10,000 animals.

The pronghorn antelope is claimed to be one of the fastest land animals in the world reaching a speed of 60 miles per hour, and for an animal with four legs that is mighty fast. Today's picture of a male pronghorn was taken near Brooks, Alberta. We were traveling west when I spotted three or four antelope out on a piece of open prairie. This fine buck was lying down by itself. We were able to locate a nearby side road off the highway and parked the car in a secluded spot. Then with a 250 mm lens mounted on the camera and with the wind blowing lightly in a direction that wouldn't carry my scent to the pronghorn I began to approach very slowly.

The animal looked so beautiful resting there! The sun was illuminating its white and tan colors, and its horns sweeping up in a graceful arc over its head gave it a most majestic bearing. Step by step I drew closer and closer until I was in perfect range for the lens. I got three shots before the pronghorn suddenly leaped to its feet. It didn't run immediately but stood there staring as I clicked the shutter two or three more times. Then as if to say, "enough is enough," it decided to take off, at first in a slow, graceful trot; then it broke into a swift, easy gallop and quickly disappeared over a rise in the direction of its friends. I was left there standing alone, but very pleased.

Both sexes of pronghorns are colored alike except the buck has a black mark down the back of the jaw and also a black band extending below the eyes to the nose.

The horns of the pronghorn are quite different from the antlers of a deer. The pronghorn has true horns; that is to say the bony core is covered with a horny sheath.

An interesting note about pronghorn antelope is that they possess a number of scent glands. These are located on different parts of the body. A pair is located on the jaw, one at the base of each horn, one on the lower back, one on each hind leg near the hock and one between the toes of each hoof. Another pair of scent glands is present on the rump patch. These glands are mainly used for communication or during sexual behavior in the autumn rutting period.

Switching from mammals to birds, Fred Lahrman of the Royal Saskatchewan Museum and I had an interesting experience with hummingbirds in August. We were sitting on the deck of my home at Last

Mountain Lake. A couple of ruby-throated hummingbirds were making steady trips to a sugar-water feeder that I had hung up for them some 10 or 12 feet away. By straining our ears we could hear the steady humming noise of their wings as they hovered in the air and sipped the moisture from the feeder. Fred wondered if this sound could be recorded on a tape machine. If captured it would indeed be a unique sound of nature. I had a cassette recorder, so we decided to give it a try. We fastened the microphone on a post support about two feet away from the feeder and then ran the machine power cord to an extension that would lead into the house. So by setting the machine at record, all we had to do when the hummer arrived was to plug the cord into a wall socket and the machine (we hoped) would record the hum of the hummer's wings. On that first attempt everything worked fine, except when we played the tapes back all we got was the roar of a truck passing by and no hint of a hum at all.

At that distance we decided the mike wasn't sensitive enough to pick up the sound, so we fastened it directly to the cord that suspended the feeder. This would bring it to a distance of eight inches from the bird. Once again we retreated into the house and once again the hummer came. In fact it came twice and we recorded twice. This time no traffic passed by on the road and to our delight we got a perfect sound recording of a hummingbird in full hovering flight. One has to hear it to appreciate it. It's truly unique.